It's another great book from CGP...

Whichever subject you're doing, it's really important to use
spelling, punctuation and grammar correctly in your writing.

Happily, this CGP book explains all those vital skills as clearly as possible,
at exactly the level you'll need for Key Stage 3 (ages 11-14).

CGP — still the best! ☺

Our sole aim here at CGP is to produce the highest quality books —
carefully written, immaculately presented and dangerously close to being funny.

Then we work our socks off to get them out to you
— at the cheapest possible prices.

Contents

Section Four — Grammar: Basics

Section Five — Grammar: Tenses

Section Six — Writing Advice

Published by CGP

Editors:
Heather McClelland
Anthony Muller
Matt Topping

With thanks to Glenn Rogers and Nicola Woodfin for the proofreading.

ISBN: 978 1 84762 407 9

Clipart from Corel®
Printed by Elanders Ltd, Newcastle upon Tyne.

Based on the classic CGP style created by Richard Parsons.

Introduction to SPaG

Writing correctly is an important skill, no matter what subjects you're studying. This book will help you master spelling, punctuation and grammar. So let's get started...

SPaG stands for Spelling, Punctuation & Grammar

1) Good SPaG is all about using accurate English in your work — you need to know how to spell properly, punctuate correctly and avoid grammatical mistakes to do well.

2) This book will help you learn all about spelling, punctuation and grammar — it's crammed full of SPaG rules, examples of good SPaG and helpful advice on how to remember it all.

The wrong kind of SPaG.

SPaG is important

1) SPaG is important because it makes your writing easier to read — it will help the reader understand what you're writing about.

Bad SPaG

i want too eat grandpa says tom ✗

With bad SPaG, it's not clear what's happening — it sounds like Tom is saying he wants to eat his grandpa.

Good SPaG

"I want to eat, Grandpa," said Tom. ✓

With good SPaG, things become a lot clearer — Tom is telling his grandpa he wants to eat.

2) You should always make sure you're using SPaG correctly in your written work, as you may get extra marks for using SPaG correctly, or lose marks if you get them wrong.

3) Using correct SPaG will become even more important as you progress through school, so the sooner you get the hang of it, the better. If you master SPaG now, you won't have to worry about it so much in the future.

There are things you can do to improve your SPaG

1) There are lots of things you can do to improve your SPaG — working through this book is a good start.

2) The best way to improve your SPaG is to read as much as possible. Books and newspaper articles normally use correct SPaG, so you'll start to recognise the spellings of words and notice punctuation patterns.

3) If you come across any unfamiliar words, look them up in a dictionary. Keep a vocabulary list to make sure you remember how to spell new words.

4) Looking through old school work will help you see whether you keep making the same types of mistakes. Once you know what you struggle with, you can focus on improving it. Jot down any words, grammar or punctuation that need work in a notebook.

SPaG — not bolognese, but the extra marks are tasty...

So that's a quick introduction to the wonderful world of SPaG. All that's left to do is to turn over and start learning. Work your way through this book, follow our advice, and you'll be laughing...

Section One — Spelling Rules

Plurals

If something is 'plural', it means that there's more than one of them.

Most words add '-s' to make them plural

For most nouns, you only need to add '-s' on the end to get the plural.

singer ➡ singer**s**   lion ➡ lion**s**   example ➡ example**s**

Some words need '-es'

If you can talk about more than one of something, you know that the word is a noun (see p.38).

Some word endings mean you have to add '-es'.

 -_CH_   -_SH_   -_S_   -_X_

mousta_ch_**ES**   eyela_sh_**ES**   glas_s_**ES**   fo_x_**ES**

Learn these special word endings, and you'll know exactly when to use '-es'.

Words ending in a vowel then '-y' just need an '-s'

If a word ends with a vowel (A, E, I, O, U) followed by a 'y' — just add an '-s' to get the plural.

birthdays   jockeys   cowboys   guys

So, if it's a vowel then a '-y', you do the normal thing — add an '-s'.

Words ending in a consonant then '-y' are trickier

For any words ending with a consonant (any letter that isn't a vowel) followed by a 'y' — drop the 'y' and add '-ies'.

The only exception to this is names — one Henry, two Henrys.

fly ➡ fl**ies**   allergy ➡ allerg**ies**   baby ➡ bab**ies**

party ➡ part**ies**   berry ➡ berr**ies**   city ➡ cit**ies**

lady ➡ lad**ies**   army ➡ arm**ies**   celebrity ➡ celebrit**ies**

The plural of plural is plurals...

Fact. Most plurals are really easy — you just add '-s'. But if the word has one of the special endings (or, even worse, it ends with a 'y'), stop, take a deep breath, and remember the rules...

Plurals

Here's another page on <u>plurals</u>. Well, we had to have more than one...

Words that end in 'o' can be tricky

There aren't many words that <u>end in 'o'</u>.
For most words that do, just <u>add '-s'</u> to get the plural.

| rhinos | photos | shampoos | radios | zoos | kangaroos |

There are a few <u>exceptions</u> though. <u>Learn</u> the most common ones:

| potatoes | tomatoes | heroes | echoes |

Most words ending with 'f' or 'fe' add '-ves'

To make a word <u>ending in 'f'</u> or <u>'fe'</u> plural, drop the '<u>f</u>' or '<u>fe</u>' and <u>add '-ves'</u>.

loaf ⟹ loaves   knife ⟹ knives   wife ⟹ wives

shelf ⟹ shelves   wolf ⟹ wolves   thief ⟹ thieves

EXCEPTION ALERT   There are some words that <u>break this rule</u> — you'll just have to <u>learn them</u>.

| chiefs | beliefs | roofs | cliffs | chefs |

There are some odd ones you need to learn

There are some words that <u>don't follow any</u> of these rules.

man ⟹ men   child ⟹ children   tooth ⟹ teeth

woman ⟹ women   mouse ⟹ mice   foot ⟹ feet

The names of <u>some animals</u> stay the <u>same</u> in the plural.

 deer   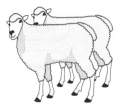 sheep    fish

Learning plurals — it's exceptionally interesting...

Like a lot of SPaG, <u>knowing the rules</u> means you'll get things right nine times out of ten.
To get things right <u>all the time</u> you need to learn those pesky <u>exceptions</u> — so get cracking.

Prefixes and Suffixes

Prefixes and suffixes change what a word means. Prefixes go at the start of words and suffixes go at the end. Remembering that 'pre' means 'before' should stop you getting confused...

Prefixes *and* suffixes *are used to make* new words

1) Prefixes and suffixes are letters that usually don't make sense by themselves. They're added to words to change the word's meaning.

2) Prefixes are things like 'un-', 're-', 'non-', 'de-' and 'dis-'. They go in front of a root word.

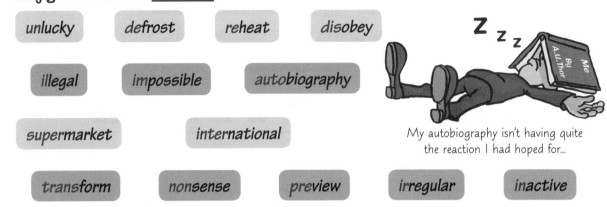

unlucky   defrost   reheat   disobey

illegal   impossible   autobiography

supermarket   international

transform   nonsense   preview   irregular   inactive

My autobiography isn't having quite the reaction I had hoped for...

3) Suffixes are things like '-ful', '-ing', '-ed', '-ment' and '-er'. They go after a root word.

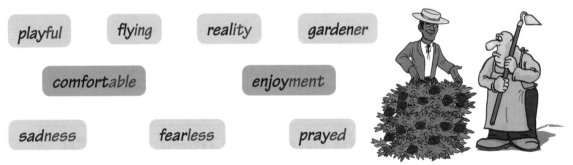

playful   flying   reality   gardener

comfortable   enjoyment

sadness   fearless   prayed

The suffix '-ful' can be confusing. It's always spelt with only one 'l' — e.g. hopeful.

Prefixes *don't change* the *spelling* of root words

The spelling of the root word never changes when a prefix is added.

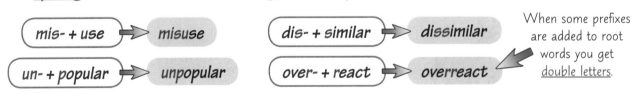

mis- + use ➡ misuse

un- + popular ➡ unpopular

dis- + similar ➡ dissimilar

over- + react ➡ overreact

When some prefixes are added to root words you get double letters.

Don't get your fixes in a twist...

You can even use some suffixes (like '-ate', '-ise' and '-ify') to turn nouns and adjectives into verbs. For example, commentate, modernise and solidify. Clever little suffixes...

Suffixes

Suffixes can mess around with spelling. Good job I'm here to explain how...

Learn these rules for words ending in 'e'

1) If a root word ends in 'e', and the first letter of the suffix is a vowel (A, E, I, O, U), you need to drop the 'e'.

achieve + -able ⟹ achievable

care + -er ⟹ carer

reverse + -ible ⟹ reversible

2) If a root word ends in 'e' and the first letter of the suffix is a consonant, keep the 'e'.

love + -ly ⟹ lovely

hope + -ful ⟹ hopeful

care + -less ⟹ careless

achieve + -ment ⟹ achievement

> **THERE ARE SOME EXCEPTIONS TO THIS RULE:**
> argue- + -ment ⟹ argument   horrible- + -ly ⟹ horribly
> true- + -ly ⟹ truly   gentle- + -ly ⟹ gently

Be careful adding a suffix to words ending with 'y'

1) If a root word ends with a consonant and then a 'y', you almost always change the 'y' to an 'i' before adding a suffix...

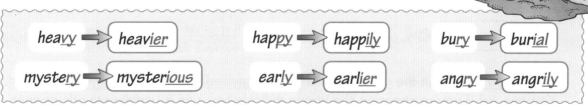

heavy ⟹ heavier   happy ⟹ happily   bury ⟹ burial

mystery ⟹ mysterious   early ⟹ earlier   angry ⟹ angrily

2) ... unless the suffix is '-ing':   cry ⟹ crying   worry ⟹ worrying

3) If the letter before 'y' is a vowel, you leave the 'y' as it is.

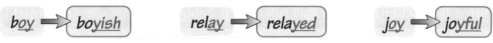

boy ⟹ boyish   relay ⟹ relayed   joy ⟹ joyful

Hurrah — no more suffering over suffixes...

Compound words are a bit like prefixes and suffixes, except they're words made up of two words that have been joined together to form a new word, like 'ladybird' and 'bedtime'. To work out how to spell a compound word, break it down into two separate words, and that should make it easier.

Suffixes

Sometimes I read a word and I think I'm <u>seeing double</u>. I blame those tricky <u>double letters</u>...

With some suffixes you need to double a letter

1) There's a <u>neat trick</u> to working out if you need to <u>double letters</u> when <u>adding a suffix</u>.

2) If the <u>suffix</u> you're adding <u>begins</u> with a <u>vowel</u>, like '<u>-ed</u>' or '<u>-ing</u>', then you usually have to <u>double the last letter</u>.

There are some <u>exceptions</u> — the letters 'c', 'h', 'k', 'q', 'w', 'x' and 'y' are <u>rarely</u> (or never) <u>doubled</u> when a <u>suffix</u> is <u>added</u>.

You only double a letter for certain words

This 'rule' <u>only works</u> if:

1) The <u>root word ends</u> in a <u>single consonant</u>...

   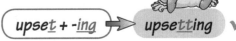

   'Jump' ends in a <u>two consonants</u>, so you <u>don't</u> double the final letter.   ✓

2) ... AND the <u>last syllable</u> is <u>stressed</u>.

A <u>syllable</u> is a part of a word which can be said in a <u>single sound</u>, e.g. "family" has <u>three</u> syllables, "<u>fam-i-ly</u>".

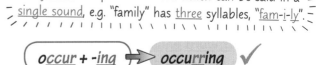

   The <u>first syllable</u> of 'offer' is <u>stressed</u>, so you don't double the last letter.   ✓

A <u>stressed syllable</u> is the <u>syllable</u> which is <u>emphasised</u> when you <u>say the word aloud</u>. You can tell if you're stressing the <u>wrong syllable</u> because it usually <u>sounds strange</u>.

PHOtograph   Pho**TOG**raphy   Photo**GRAPH**ic ⬅ This shows how the <u>stressed syllable</u> can <u>move</u> in similar words.

There are a few EXCEPTIONS to this rule: E.g. re<u>boot</u> + <u>-ed</u> ➡ reboo<u>t</u>ed

It's either a double letter or my keyboard's got stuck...

<u>Double letters</u> can <u>change</u> the entire <u>meaning</u> of what you want to say. Imagine '<u>hopping</u>' for Christmas presents instead of '<u>hoping</u>' for them — you'd look a bit <u>silly</u> doing that.

Comparing Things

When you want to <u>compare</u> things you need to use <u>comparatives</u> — the clue's in the name.

Comparatives say what's bigger, better or worse

<u>Comparatives</u> are words which can be used to <u>compare</u> two things.

> Sarah is <u>taller</u> than Hassan.   Hassan is <u>shorter</u> than Sarah.

These are <u>comparatives</u> — they compare the heights of Hassan and Sarah.

There are two ways to compare things

1) For <u>short words</u> like 'smart' and 'slow', stick the <u>suffix</u> '<u>-er</u>' on the <u>end</u>, and then add '<u>than</u>'.

> Dogs are <u>smarter than</u> cats.   Stefan is <u>slower than</u> Jane.

Well, I'm short. Why can't they add er to me?

2) For <u>longer words</u> you need to put '<u>more</u>' or '<u>less</u>' in <u>front</u>, and '<u>than</u>' <u>afterwards</u>.

> Bob is <u>less</u> cheerful <u>than</u> Anka.   Amelle is <u>more</u> interesting <u>than</u> Valerie.

Some words do their own thing

1) You <u>can't</u> add '-er' or 'more/less' to <u>all words</u>. Some words change to a <u>special comparing</u> word:

good → better   bad → worse   little → less   much / many → more

2) You will still normally <u>need</u> to use '<u>than</u>' with these words for them to <u>make sense</u>:

> Fred's handwriting is <u>better than</u> Julia's.   The painting is <u>worse than</u> the photo.

> I have <u>less than</u> he does.

Oi!

> She has collected <u>more than</u> seven hundred autographs.

You're more intelligent now you've read this page...

This stuff is great if you want to say you're <u>better</u> at something <u>than</u> your mate or if you want to <u>use comparatives</u> correctly, which is <u>more useful than</u> a chocolate teapot, as I'm sure you'll agree.

Saying Something is the Most or Least

This is the <u>best</u>, the <u>most</u> amusing and the <u>least</u> dull page in the book. (I'm the <u>biggest</u> liar.)

Superlatives *say what's* biggest, best *or* worst

1) To say something is the <u>most</u> of something, you can put '<u>-est</u>' on the <u>end</u> of the word.

2) You can <u>only</u> do this to <u>short words</u> or words that <u>end in 'y'</u>.

I'm the <u>fastest</u> runner at my school.   *Your dog is the <u>cutest</u>.*

Sue is the <u>trendiest</u> girl in class. ← The 'y' in trendy <u>changes</u> to 'i' — '-est' is a <u>suffix</u>, so it follows <u>suffix</u> spelling rules (see p.5-6).

Use 'most' or 'least' *with* longer words

1) <u>Longer words</u> sound weird if you add '<u>-est</u>'. Instead you need to use '<u>most</u>'.

She is <u>the most interesting</u> chemistry teacher ever.

Dave is <u>the most hilarious</u> person I know.

2) To say something has the <u>smallest</u> amount of <u>something</u>, use '<u>least</u>' instead of '<u>most</u>'.

Lucas had <u>the least success</u> in the contest.   *Zola is <u>the least careful</u>.*

In most sentences, you have to use '<u>the</u>' with '<u>most</u>' or '<u>least</u>' or it won't <u>make sense</u>.

> Never use 'most' and '-est' together — it doesn't <u>make sense</u>.
> And <u>DON'T</u> say <u>bestest</u> — it isn't a proper word.

There are some *exceptions*

Some words <u>don't</u> use '<u>-est</u>' or '<u>most/least</u>'. You need to <u>learn</u> these <u>special superlatives</u>:

bad ⟶ worst   good ⟶ best   little ⟶ least   much / many ⟶ most

Jaffa is <u>the worst</u> cat.   *I won <u>the least</u> amount of money.*

English is her <u>best</u> subject.   *They have <u>the most</u> tasty pizzas.*

CGP's jokes are the most fun...

Another page down, another lesson <u>learnt</u>. The main thing to <u>avoid</u> here is using <u>two superlatives</u> together. Saying things like 'the <u>most bestest</u>' will make you sound like a <u>wally</u>, so don't do it.

Silent Letters and Unstressed Vowels

Silent letters are mighty important, but also mighty annoying because they're, well... silent.
This page is worth its weight in gold when it comes to having good spelling, so read on...

Some words have *silent letters*

1) Silent letters are letters which you can't hear when you say the word aloud.
This makes words with silent letters tricky to spell.

2) You've got no choice but to learn the spellings of common words
with silent letters so you don't get caught out.

Shhhhhhh!

Learn the *correct spelling* of these words

| scene | science | conscience | scissors |
| scent | muscle | descend | fascinate |

| kneel | knife | knight | knock |
| knot | know | knowledge | knit |

Silent 'b'

| lamb | debt | tomb | subtle |
| doubt | bomb | comb | |

Silent 'h'

| which | whether | when | while | whistle |
| hour | chemist | ghost | honest | school |

| write | whole | wrong |
| two | answer | who |

| listen | Christmas |
| castle | fasten |

| should | could | would |
| half | calm | walk | talk |

Some vowel sounds *make words hard to spell*

In some words, the vowel sound isn't clear — these are called unstressed vowels.
These words can be hard to spell because the vowels don't make the sound you expect.
Here are some useful examples for you to learn:

private	separate	definitely	doctor	easily	parliament
difference	government	describe	biscuit	frighten	vegetable
company	general	ridiculous	animal	factory	desperate

I'm AT a privATe party...

No really, I am. Making up funny sentences can help you remember how to spell these words —
things like 'there's a rat in separate' or 'U and I eat biscuits'. Mmmm, biscuits...

Hard and Soft 'c' Sounds

Words with <u>hard</u> or <u>soft</u> '<u>c</u>' <u>sounds</u> can be <u>tricky to spell</u>, so take a look at this page...

A hard 'c' is one that sounds like a 'k'

When you're spelling a word with a <u>hard 'c' sound</u>, you need to know whether to use <u>c</u>, <u>k</u> or <u>ch</u>. There's <u>no rule</u> for this — you just have to <u>learn</u> the <u>correct spellings</u>.

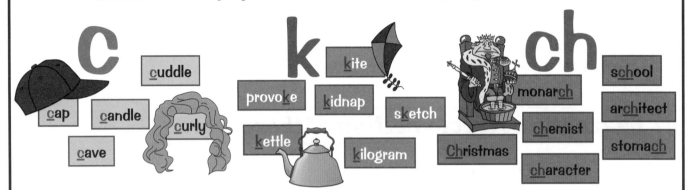

A soft 'c' is one that sounds like an 's'

<u>Soft 'c' sounds</u> can make you want to write an '<u>s</u>' when you need a '<u>c</u>' instead.

Here are some common <u>examples</u> to <u>learn</u>:

> You <u>only</u> really need to <u>think</u> about whether an '<u>s</u>' sound is a <u>soft 'c'</u> when it's <u>followed</u> by an '<u>e</u>', '<u>i</u>' or '<u>y</u>' — it's very <u>rare</u> that a soft 'c' is followed by any <u>other letter</u>.

medi<u>c</u>ine	re<u>c</u>ipe	sli<u>c</u>e	<u>c</u>ity	<u>c</u>entre	sau<u>c</u>e	senten<u>c</u>e
re<u>c</u>ent	<u>c</u>ellar	<u>c</u>ircus	<u>c</u>entury	mi<u>c</u>e	sin<u>c</u>ere	convin<u>c</u>e
<u>c</u>eiling	<u>c</u>ircle	<u>c</u>emetery	prin<u>c</u>ess	offi<u>c</u>e	ex<u>c</u>eed	de<u>c</u>imal

A soft 'c' can change how you add suffixes

1) If you're <u>adding</u> a <u>suffix</u> to a <u>root word</u> which <u>ends</u> in a <u>soft 'c'</u> and then an '<u>e</u>' — you <u>don't drop</u> the '<u>e</u>'...

> You do the same if there is a <u>soft 'g'</u> sound just before the '<u>-e</u>' in the <u>root word</u>, e.g. knowled<u>ge</u>able.

(noti<u>ce</u> + -<u>able</u>) ➔ notic<u>eable</u>   (servi<u>ce</u> + -<u>able</u>) ➔ servic<u>eable</u>

2) ... <u>unless</u> the suffix <u>starts</u> with an '<u>e</u>' or '<u>i</u>'.

(noti<u>ce</u> + -<u>ing</u>) ➔ noti<u>cing</u>   (servi<u>ce</u> + -<u>ing</u>) ➔ servi<u>cing</u>

'C' sounds think they're hard, but we're ready for 'em...

When it comes to words with <u>hard</u> and <u>soft 'c' sounds</u>, it's a real case of sitting down and <u>learning</u> how to <u>spell</u> them. So, come on — grab a pen and paper and let's get them well and truly learnt.

i Before e Rule

The 'i before e rule' isn't perfect, so it's a good idea to learn how to spell common words that use 'ie' or 'ei', so you'll always be prepared with the correct spellings. Anyway, the rule goes:

> 'i' before 'e' except after 'c', but only when it rhymes with bee.

When it rhymes with bee, it's 'i' before 'e'...

Think about whether the 'ie' sound in the word rhymes with 'bee'. If it does it's 'i before e'.

piece   chief   field
thief   hygiene
niece
diesel   believe   achieve

The whole word doesn't need to rhyme with bee — just the 'ie' sound.

...except after 'c'

If the 'ie' sound rhymes with bee and comes after a 'c', it will be 'ei'.

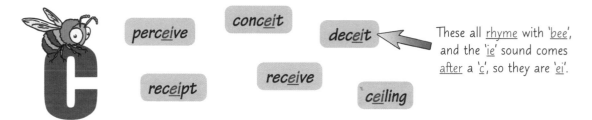

perceive   conceit   deceit
receipt   receive
ceiling

These all rhyme with 'bee', and the 'ie' sound comes after a 'c', so they are 'ei'.

If it doesn't rhyme with bee, it's 'e' before 'i'

It's 'ei' when the sound doesn't rhyme with bee. Learn these examples.

eight	weight	neighbour	foreign
vein	their	veil	sleigh
heir	rein	forfeit	weird

Wasp

These don't rhyme with 'bee', so they are spelt 'ei'.

Bee a good student — learn these examples...

The 'i before e rule' is definitely a tricky one to get your head round, but make sure you take the time to get it learnt. Once you've got it sorted, those pesky 'ie' words will be much easier to spell.

i Before e Rule

More of the same here I'm afraid. This stuff <u>carries on</u> from the <u>previous page</u>...

It's 'ie' if it doesn't rhyme with bee, and it's after 'c'

There are only a few examples to learn here:

  ancient   society   science    conscience

Learn the exceptions to the rules

There are <u>always</u> exceptions to the rules — you need to <u>learn</u> them off by heart:

DIET **EXCEPTIONS** SEIZE

SPECIES   FRIEND

Another exception is <u>people's names</u>, like K<u>ei</u>th.

Ignore the rule when you add a prefix or a suffix

When you add a <u>prefix</u> or a <u>suffix</u> to a word you can ignore the
'<u>i before e rule</u>' even if the new word seems to <u>break</u> the rule:

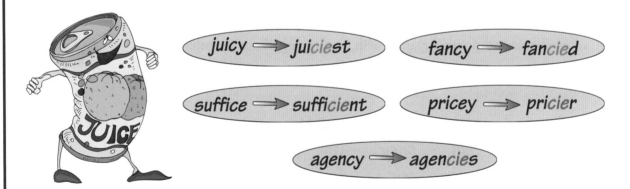

juicy ➡ juiciest   fancy ➡ fancied

suffice ➡ sufficient   pricey ➡ pricier

agency ➡ agencies

The <u>prefix</u> and <u>suffix spelling rules</u> (see p.4-6) are <u>more important</u> than the 'i before e rule'.

The 'i before e rule' — as clear as mud on a rainy day...

This stuff makes my brain <u>hurt</u> a bit. If you get it, that's <u>marvellous</u>, but if you're finding it <u>tricky</u>, make sure you learn <u>all the words</u> on these pages (yep, ALL of them), so you don't come <u>unstuck</u>.

Revision Summary Questions

Now that you've gobbled up all of the information from this section, I'm going to test what you've learnt. Don't worry, it won't hurt... too much. If you find any of these questions too tricky, check back in the section for some helpful guidance. When you're done, you can take a look at the answers at the back of the book.

1) Turn these words into plurals by adding '-s' or '-es':
   a) house   b) fox   c) glass   d) church   e) carrot

2) Make these words plural:
   a) berry   b) day   c) boy   d) baby   e) party

3) Write down the plurals of:
   a) radio   b) photo   c) tomato   d) hero   e) rhino

4) Change these 'f' and 'fe' ending words into their plural forms:
   a) loaf   b) belief   c) wife   d) thief   e) knife

5) Make these words plural:
   a) sheep   b) child   c) woman   d) goose   e) tooth

6) Add the prefixes in brackets to each of the words below:
   a) (im) perfect   b) (ir) relevant   c) (re) use   d) (il) literate   e) (un) necessary

7) Add the suffixes in brackets to each of the following words:
   a) cheer (ful)   b) value (able)   c) care (ful)   d) sense (ible)   e) common (ly)

8) Turn these adjectives into adverbs by adding '-ly'.
   a) happy   b) soft   c) gentle   d) funny   e) normal

9) Add the suffixes in brackets to each of the following words:
   a) envy (ous)   b) mercy (ful)   c) delay (ed)   d) funny (er)   e) try (ing)

10) Add the suffixes in brackets to each of the words below. Watch out for double letters.
   a) thin (er)   b) dump (ed)   c) talk (ing)   d) challenge (er)   e) chat (ing)

11) Rewrite these sentences so that the underlined comparatives and superlatives are correct:
   a) My dog is the baddest dog at puppy training. Hopefully he'll behave gooder one day.
   b) Sayid is more tall than Herbert, but he eats least than him.

12) Circle the correct spelling of each of the words below:
   a) scissors / sissors   c) gost / ghost   e) anser / answer
   b) knowledge / nowledge   d) whistle / whisle   f) bom / bomb

13) Circle the correct spelling of each of the words below:
   a) doctor / docter   c) frightoned / frightened   e) governmant / government
   b) private / privite   d) animul / animal   f) biscit / biscuit

14) Circle the correct spelling of each of the words below:
   a) sity / city   b) circle / sircle   c) muscle / mussle   d) scentury / century

15) Rewrite the passage below with the correct spellings:
   Our TV broke, so we took it back to the shop with the reciept. We got a new one (big enough to reach the cieling), but the next day a theif broke in and stole it. I can't beleive our luck!

16) Find the 8 spelling errors in this passage and correct them:
   Mike, my best freind, is great, but he's also really wierd and he's begining to get on my nerves. He loves celebritys and talks about them all the time at scool, espesially when we're in sience — it's very distractting.

Commonly Misused Words

This <u>may be</u> an interesting page, but then again <u>maybe</u> not. <u>Anyway</u>, I'll let you decide...

Don't confuse 'maybe' and 'may be'...

1) '<u>Maybe</u>' is one word, but '<u>may be</u>' is two words — they mean <u>different things</u>.

2) '<u>Maybe</u>' is an <u>adverb</u> (see p.47) which means '<u>perhaps</u>'.

> *<u>Maybe</u> our teacher's an alien.*   ⟵ This means that <u>perhaps</u> their teacher is an alien.

3) '<u>May be</u>' is a <u>verb phrase</u> which means '<u>might be</u>'.

> *Twelve handbags <u>may be</u> more than you need.*

> *Twelve handbags <u>might be</u> more than you need.*   ⟵ Try <u>replacing</u> '<u>may be</u>' with '<u>might be</u>' and seeing if the sentence still <u>makes sense</u>. If it does then you're using the right one.

'Anyway' and 'anybody' are both one word

1) '<u>Anyway</u>' is an <u>adverb</u> (see p.47) which means '<u>regardless</u>' — it's spelt as <u>one word</u>.

> *Walt had a cold, but Clara went on holiday <u>anyway</u>.*   ⟵ This means that Clara went on holiday <u>regardless</u> of Walt's health.

2) '<u>Any way</u>' is <u>two separate</u> words and it means '<u>any means</u>'.

> This is asking if there is <u>any means</u> of changing the TV channel. ⟶ *Is there <u>any way</u> to change the TV channel?*

3) '<u>Everybody</u>' is a <u>pronoun</u> (see p.40) which means '<u>every person</u>' — it's spelt as <u>one word</u>.

> *Where is <u>everybody</u>?*   ⟵ This is asking where <u>all the people</u> are.

4) '<u>Every body</u>' means '<u>every physical body</u>' — it's <u>two separate words</u>.

> *<u>Every body</u> shape is unique.*   ⟵ In this sentence '<u>every body</u>' means '<u>every physical body</u>'.

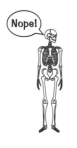
Nope!

Is there any body there?

> Watch out for '<u>anybody</u>' and '<u>any body</u>' too. '<u>Anybody</u>' means '<u>any person</u>', '<u>any body</u>' means '<u>any physical body</u>'.

Everybody and anybody can get this right...

Once you've got the hang of the <u>different meanings</u> to these words, spelling them will be a doddle. When you come across them, stop and think about whether you need <u>two words</u> or <u>one word</u>.

Commonly Misused Words

Let's get to grips with when we need <u>two words</u> and when we only need <u>one word</u>.

'No one' is two words but 'nobody' is one word

1) You must always write '<u>no one</u>' as <u>two words</u>. Writing '<u>noone</u>' is <u>wrong</u> — don't do it.

> <u>No one</u> knew what they were doing.   <u>No one</u> ate the jellyfish pie.

2) '<u>Nobody</u>' is also <u>one word</u> (when you want it to mean <u>no one</u>).

> <u>Nobody</u> won the tiddlywinks contest.

3) Other words for talking <u>about people</u> are <u>one word</u> too. E.g. '<u>everyone</u>', '<u>someone</u>' and '<u>anyone</u>'.

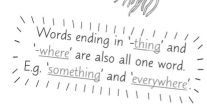

Words ending in '<u>-thing</u>' and '<u>-where</u>' are also all one word. E.g. '<u>something</u>' and '<u>everywhere</u>'.

'Into' and 'in to' mean different things

1) Use '<u>into</u>' when something is <u>moving towards</u> the <u>inside</u> of <u>something</u>.

> The dog ran <u>into</u> the cave.
> The dog ran <u>inside</u> the cave.

If you can <u>swap</u> '<u>into</u>' with '<u>inside</u>' and the sentence still makes <u>sense</u>, you're using '<u>into</u>' <u>correctly</u>.

2) You also use '<u>into</u>' when you're talking about something '<u>turning into</u>' something else.

> We <u>changed into</u> our costumes.   He <u>turned into</u> a monster.

3) The rest of the time '<u>in</u>' and '<u>to</u>' are two separate words:

> They came <u>in to</u> speak to Jill.   The ants marched <u>in to</u> steal the sugar.

'A lot' and 'thank you' are always two words

1) A <u>common mistake</u> to is to write '<u>alot</u>' instead of '<u>a lot</u>' — 'alot' is <u>never correct</u>.

> I don't have <u>a lot</u> of money.   We've got <u>a lot</u> of homework to do.

2) '<u>Thank you</u>' should <u>never</u> be written as one word.

> <u>Thank you</u> for looking after my rabbits.

This page'll turn you into a SPaG whizz...

'<u>Into</u>' and '<u>in to</u>' can get you in a muddle if you <u>mix them up</u>. E.g. 'She turned her homework <u>in to</u> her teacher' means something <u>quite different</u> to 'She turned her homework <u>into</u> her teacher'.

Commonly Misused Words

You'll have to <u>practise</u> a bit to <u>pass</u> any spelling tests you might have — I'm full of good <u>advice</u>.

'In fact' is two words, not one

'<u>In fact</u>' is another example of a phrase that is always written as <u>two</u> separate <u>words</u>:

Writing '<u>infact</u>' is never right.

> I don't hate bugs; <u>in fact</u> I love them.

'Practise' is a verb, but 'practice' is a noun

1) '<u>Practise</u>' is a <u>doing word</u> — it's spelt with an '<u>s</u>'.

> I often practi<u>s</u>e playing the piano.   Mr Smith likes to practi<u>s</u>e tap dancing.

2) '<u>Practice</u>' is a <u>noun</u> — it's spelt with a '<u>c</u>'.

> I've got cricket practi<u>c</u>e tonight.   Football practi<u>c</u>e has been cancelled.

It's the same with other words too

1) '<u>Advise</u>' and '<u>license</u>' are <u>verbs</u>, which means they're spelt with an '<u>s</u>'.

> Mohammed advi<u>s</u>ed Liz to avoid lions.   The shop isn't licen<u>s</u>ed to sell gum.

Advise and <u>license</u> are things that we <u>do</u>.

2) '<u>Advice</u>' and '<u>licence</u>' are <u>nouns</u>, which means they're spelt with a '<u>c</u>'.

> Mohammed gave Liz some advi<u>c</u>e.   Mr Cool has a licen<u>c</u>e to chill.

Don't confuse 'passed' with 'past'

1) '<u>Passed</u>' with '<u>-ed</u>' is an <u>action</u> — it has to be <u>done</u> by <u>someone</u> or <u>something</u>.

> Marvin <u>passed</u> the parcel to Tamina.   We <u>passed</u> the zoo on the way to school.

Marvin <u>did the passing</u> — 'passed' is the <u>past tense</u> of the verb '<u>to pass</u>'.

2) '<u>Past</u>' with '<u>-t</u>' is <u>never</u> an action.

> Our rocket flew <u>past</u> the moon.   In the <u>past</u> houses didn't have electricity.

In this sentence '<u>past</u>' describes <u>where</u> the rocket went.   Here, '<u>past</u>' describes a <u>period of time</u>.

I practise juggling whilst advising cats about rats...

These words can be a right pain, but <u>getting them wrong</u> can make your work really <u>hard to read</u>.

Section Two — Common Spelling Mistakes

Commonly Misused Words

This book is bound to have a positive <u>effect</u> on your spelling...

'Affect' is the action, but 'effect' is the result

1) '<u>Affect</u>' is a <u>verb</u> — it's an <u>action</u> which <u>influences</u> something else.

> *A poor diet can <u>a</u>ffect your fitness.* ⇐ A poor diet is <u>doing</u> something to your fitness.

2) '<u>Effect</u>' is a <u>noun</u> — it's the <u>result</u> of an <u>action</u>.

> *A poor diet has an <u>e</u>ffect on your fitness.* ⇐ This is talking about the <u>result</u> of a poor diet.

'Accept' is totally different from 'except'

1) '<u>Accept</u>' is a <u>verb</u> — it means to '<u>agree</u>' with something or to '<u>receive</u>' something.

> *Most pupils <u>accept</u> that they have to do their homework.* ⇐ This means that most pupils <u>agree</u> that they have to do their homework.

2) '<u>Except</u>' means '<u>not including</u>'.

This means that <u>only</u> Boris doesn't do his homework. ⇒ *All the pupils do their homework <u>except</u> Boris.*

'Where', 'were' and 'wear' have different meanings

These words <u>sound</u> and <u>look</u> a bit similar, but they have very <u>different</u> meanings.

1) '<u>Where</u>' is used for <u>places</u> and <u>positions</u>.

> *I don't know <u>where</u> I've put my pencil case.*   *<u>Where</u> is Cairo?*

I'm heading that way if you want a ride.

2) '<u>Were</u>' is the <u>past form</u> of '<u>are</u>'.

> *We <u>were</u> fishing by the lake.*   *They <u>were</u> fighting over the last chip.*

3) '<u>We're</u>' is the <u>shortened form</u> of '<u>we are</u>'.

> *<u>We're</u> off to fly a kite.*   *<u>We're</u> going to the fair.*   *<u>We're</u> the best.*

4) '<u>Wear</u>' is what you do with <u>clothes</u>, <u>shoes</u> and <u>jewellery</u>.

> *I <u>wear</u> my trainers for P.E.*   *I <u>wear</u> my onesie when no one is around.*

I like going to school, except on days ending in 'y'...

There are definitely some <u>confusing</u> words on this page. They might <u>sound</u> almost the <u>same</u>, but they're <u>spelt differently</u> and they have <u>different meanings</u>. Don't let them fool you.

Commonly Misused Words

Here are some more words that <u>sound the same</u> as each other but don't mean the same thing...

'There', 'their' and 'they're' have different meanings

These three words <u>sound alike</u>, but they're <u>spelt differently</u>.
It's really <u>easy</u> to get them <u>mixed up</u>, so pay <u>extra attention</u> to this bit.

> These are <u>homophones</u>.
> Homophones are words
> that <u>sound the same</u> but
> <u>mean different things</u>.

1) '<u>There</u>' goes with '<u>where</u>' — it's about <u>places</u> and <u>positions</u>.

> In town <u>there</u>'s a cinema.   <u>There</u> was a hole in the garden.

2) '<u>Their</u>' means '<u>belonging</u> to <u>them</u>'.

> <u>Their</u> voices could be heard outside.   <u>Their</u> tentacles were horrible.

3) '<u>They're</u>' is short for '<u>they are</u>'.

> <u>They're</u> my best friends.   They think <u>they're</u> going to win the match.

'Your' and 'you're' are like 'their' and 'they're'

'<u>Your</u>' and '<u>you're</u>' can also be tricky — add them to your list of '<u>words to watch out for</u>'.

1) '<u>Your</u>' means '<u>belonging</u> to <u>you</u>'.

> <u>Your</u> dinner is ready.   <u>Your</u> car is blocking my drive.

2) '<u>You're</u>' is short for '<u>you are</u>'.

> <u>You're</u> on the cricket team.   <u>You're</u> not going to the disco.

'Hear' and 'here' aren't the same

1) '<u>Here</u>' is the opposite of '<u>there</u>'.

> Come <u>here</u>.   <u>Here</u> they come.   I'm not <u>here</u>.

2) '<u>Hear</u>' is when you <u>listen</u>.

> I can't <u>hear</u> you.   There's an '<u>ear</u>' in '<u>hear</u>'.   Dogs can <u>hear</u> everything.

"Hear ye, hear ye, here is the opposite of there..."

We've looked at <u>seven tricky words</u> on this page. <u>Jot</u> them down and <u>try making</u> your <u>own</u> <u>sentences using</u> these <u>words</u>. When you've finished, <u>treat yourself</u> to a two-minute <u>daydream</u>.

Commonly Misused Words

Yep, you guessed it — we still need to look at some more <u>confusing words</u>.

'To' / 'Too' / 'Two' — they're all different

This one's a really <u>common mistake</u>, so make sure you don't slip up:

1) '<u>To</u>' means '<u>towards</u>' or is <u>part</u> of a <u>verb</u>.

> *I want <u>to</u> go home.*   ← In this sentence '<u>to</u>' is part of the verb '<u>to go</u>'.

> *They're going <u>to</u> the shop.*   ← In this sentence '<u>to</u>' means '<u>towards</u>'.

2) '<u>Two</u>' is just the <u>number 2</u>.

> *We won <u>two</u> thousand pounds.*

> *I saw a lion with <u>two</u> tails.*

3) '<u>Too</u>' means '<u>too much</u>' or '<u>also</u>'.

> *My hair is <u>too</u> long...*   ← This means the hair is <u>overly</u> long.

> *... and it's the wrong colour <u>too</u>.*   ← This means the hair is <u>also</u> the wrong colour.

'Off' means 'not on' — the rest of the time use 'of'

1) '<u>Off</u>' means '<u>not on</u>' or '<u>away from</u>'.

> *All shoes 10% <u>off</u>.*   ← This means 10% <u>taken away from</u> the price.

> *The TV was <u>off</u>.*   ← This means the TV was '<u>not on</u>'.

2) '<u>Of</u>' is a <u>linking word</u> — it's a preposition (see p.51).

> *The sack was full <u>of</u> presents.*

> *He's the king <u>of</u> the castle.*   ← '<u>Of</u>' links these words together.

'Our' shows possession and 'are' is a verb

1) '<u>Our</u>' means '<u>belonging</u> to <u>us</u>'.

> *That's <u>our</u> house.*

> *<u>Our</u> hamster has eaten the dog.*   ← '<u>Our</u>' shows that the hamster <u>belongs</u> to us.

2) '<u>Are</u>' is a <u>present tense form</u> of the verb '<u>to be</u>' (see p.59).

> *They <u>are</u> sad.*

> *You <u>are</u> messy.*   ← '<u>Are</u>' tells you what the subject of the verb is <u>being</u>.

A good old farmer "ooh arr" — a third our/are sound...

Take it from me, getting your head around this stuff will <u>make life</u> much <u>easier</u> in the future. Soon you'll even be able to tell others when they're getting it <u>wrong</u>. I'm sure they'd be very grateful...

Commonly Misused Words

This page has got some more words that are out to <u>trick you</u>. Don't be fooled...

Don't confuse 'though', 'through' and 'thorough'

1) '<u>Though</u>' means '<u>however</u>'.

> Going on holiday is fun, <u>though</u> flying can be stressful.

2) '<u>Through</u>' means '<u>going from one side</u> of something to the <u>other</u>'.

> We went <u>through</u> the forbidden forest.   They went <u>through</u> the stinky swamp.

3) '<u>Thorough</u>' means '<u>careful</u>'.

> My teacher found every mistake. She was very <u>thorough</u> in her marking.

Don't mix up 'piece' and 'peace'...

1) '<u>Piece</u>' means '<u>part of</u>'.

> I'd love a <u>piece</u> of cheese.   Please can I have a <u>piece</u> of cake?

2) '<u>Peace</u>' is the <u>opposite of war</u> — it means '<u>calm</u>'.

> I need a bit of <u>peace</u> and quiet.   Leave me in <u>peace</u>.

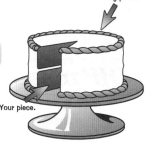

My piece.

Your piece.

...or 'whether' and 'weather'...

1) '<u>Whether</u>' means '<u>if</u>'.

> I'm not sure <u>whether</u> I'll go to the party.   I wonder <u>whether</u> dogs can fly.

2) '<u>Weather</u>' is things like <u>rain</u>, <u>clouds</u> and <u>snow</u>.

> The <u>weather</u> last weekend was awful.   I can't stand this hot <u>weather</u>.

...or 'loose' and 'lose'

1) '<u>Loose</u>' means '<u>not secure</u>'.

> My tooth is <u>loose</u>.   This screw is <u>loose</u>.   Jack's spider is <u>loose</u>.

2) '<u>Lose</u>' can mean to '<u>not win</u>' or to '<u>misplace something</u>'.

> We'll probably <u>lose</u> the match on Saturday.   Don't <u>lose</u> your phone.

Learn these words — it's a piece of cake...

Learning spellings <u>needn't be boring</u> — especially when cake's involved. Mmmm... cake.

Section Two — Common Spelling Mistakes

Commonly Misused Words

It's time to say <u>bye</u> to <u>those</u> annoying <u>spelling mistakes</u> that make <u>us</u> so <u>confused</u>.

It's easy to confuse 'buy', 'by' and 'bye'

1) '<u>Buy</u>' is what you do when you <u>pay for something</u>.

> *Tina wants to <u>buy</u> a new car.*

> *Ted went to <u>buy</u> a donkey.*

2) '<u>Bye</u>' is a shortened version of '<u>goodbye</u>'.

> *Larry shouted, "Bye, girls!"*

> *"Bye, Sanjay! See you next week!"*

3) '<u>By</u>' is a <u>linking word</u>. It usually means '<u>next to</u>' or '<u>because of</u>'.

> *We live <u>by</u> the sea.* ← This sentence means we live <u>next to</u> the sea.

> *They won <u>by</u> cheating.* ← This sentence means they won <u>because</u> they cheated.

Don't use 'them' when you mean 'those'

1) '<u>Them</u>' is a <u>pronoun</u> (see p.40). It <u>replaces</u> the <u>noun</u> you've <u>just mentioned</u>.

> *Wasps are annoying. I hate <u>them</u>.* ← 'Them' replaces 'wasps'.

Only use '<u>them</u>' if it's clear what 'them' <u>refers to</u>.

> *Hazel loves her dogs. She's always talking about <u>them</u>.* ← 'Them' replaces 'dogs'.

2) '<u>Those</u>' is used to <u>point out specific things</u>.

> *Look at <u>those</u> shoes!*

> *I don't know <u>those</u> people.*

> *<u>Those</u> pictures are terrible.*

Don't write 'us' when you mean 'me'

'<u>Me</u>' is a pronoun. We use '<u>me</u>' to talk about ourselves.

> *Hang on, give <u>me</u> a minute.*

> *Tell <u>me</u> the truth.*

> *Make <u>me</u> a cup of tea.*

You can only use '<u>us</u>' instead of '<u>me</u>' when you're talking about <u>yourself AND someone else</u>. You should <u>never</u> use '<u>us</u>' when you are <u>only</u> talking about <u>yourself</u>.

It's all about me. I mean us. I meant to say us...

There are a <u>few don'ts</u> on this page, but <u>don't think</u> we're just being <u>awkward</u> (there's another one). You need to <u>know</u> this stuff, so <u>don't</u> just ignore our advice. Learn it...

Commonly Misused Words

If you've ever found yourself <u>mixing up</u> the words '<u>teach</u>' and '<u>learn</u>', '<u>lend</u>' and '<u>borrow</u>' or even '<u>bought</u>' and '<u>brought</u>', then this is the page you've been waiting for...

Teach and learn are opposites

Kick your legs, Bob!

Can I go in the water yet?

1) <u>Teaching</u> means '<u>giving out knowledge</u>'.

    Can you <u>learn</u> me to swim? ✗

    Can you <u>teach</u> me to swim? ✓

    This <u>doesn't make sense</u> — you want the <u>other person</u> to do the <u>teaching</u>, <u>not</u> the <u>learning</u>.

    This <u>does make sense</u> — <u>you're</u> doing the <u>learning</u>; <u>they're</u> doing the <u>teaching</u>.

2) <u>Learning</u> means '<u>taking in knowledge</u>'.

    I want to <u>learn</u> Spanish.

    Ahmed is <u>learning</u> to drive.

Lend something to someone, borrow it from them

'<u>Lend</u>' and '<u>borrow</u>' are <u>opposites</u>. If I <u>lend</u> something <u>to you</u>, <u>you're borrowing</u> it <u>from me</u>.

1) <u>Lend</u> means <u>giving something out</u>.

    Will you <u>lend</u> me your binoculars?

    Rana <u>lends</u> £10 to Pam.

2) <u>Borrowing</u> means <u>taking something from someone</u>.

    Can I <u>borrow</u> your binoculars?

    Pam <u>borrows</u> £10 from Rana.

    This means Rana is <u>giving</u> the £10 and Pam is <u>receiving</u> it.

Don't mix up 'bought' and 'brought'

1) <u>Bought</u> is the <u>past tense</u> of the verb '<u>to buy</u>'. You say that <u>you've bought something</u> when you've <u>paid for it</u>.

    Jake <u>bought</u> some sweets. ⬅ This means Jake has <u>paid for</u> some sweets.

2) <u>Brought</u> is the past tense of the verb '<u>to bring</u>'. You can say that <u>you've brought something</u> when you have something <u>with you</u>.

    Jake <u>brought</u> an elephant to school. ⬅ This means Jake <u>had</u> an elephant <u>with him</u>.

Lending, borrowing — I think I'll go to the library...

You may be thinking "What's the big deal? <u>People know what I mean anyway</u>." Well, <u>they won't always</u> be able to work it out if you mix these words up. Avoid that confusion and get it right.

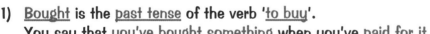

Tricky Words

Some words have <u>awkward spellings</u> and simply need to be <u>learnt</u>.

Words with double letters can be tricky

Words with <u>double letters</u> are hard to spell because <u>double letters</u> make a <u>single sound</u>.
You'll just have to learn how to <u>spell</u> these words:

accommodation	address	beginning	committee	different	disappear
eventually	exaggerate	immediately	necessary	occasion	success

Some words end in similar sounds

Words that sound like they <u>end</u> with the <u>same sound</u> aren't always spelt the same.
Watch out for these tricky endings:

-shun

electrician	attention	collision
magician	direction	confusion
optician	education	decision
politician	fiction	mansion
technician	nation	tension

-shul

essential	artificial
impartial	crucial
initial	official
residential	social
substantial	special

-shus

ambitious	conscious
cautious	delicious
contentious	ferocious
pretentious	suspicious
superstitious	vicious

Some words have tricky letter combinations...

Some letter combinations are <u>tricky</u>, but sadly they pop up time and time again. Watch out for:

qu

antique	quantity	question
banquet	quarter	queue
critique	queen	quick
quality	quest	quote

ough

bought	enough	thorough
cough	fought	thought
dough	nought	through
drought	rough	tough

gu

catalogue	guard	guilty
dialogue	guess	guitar
fatigue	quest	tongue
guarantee	guide	vague

...others are just plain awkward

It will help to make a list of words you find <u>tricky</u> to spell.
Here are some to get you started:

height	rhythm	neighbour	aeroplane	aisle	strength	Wednesday	temporary

Remember ~~the 5th of November~~ these words...

When you're <u>learning</u> these <u>spellings</u>, it'll help to think of <u>silly ways</u> to help you <u>remember</u> them.
Like <u>saying</u> the words <u>how they're spelt</u> — it might sound odd, but this could make them stick.

Revision Summary Questions

It's almost time to say goodbye to Section Two, but before you do, give these questions a go...

1) Circle the correct 'maybe' or 'may be' in each of these sentences:
   a) Maybe / May be George is a superhero.   b) That maybe / may be true.

2) Add 'anyway', 'any way', 'everybody' or 'every body' correctly to this passage:
   Is there _____ we could go to the cinema for my party? It's a great idea because
   _____ loves films. If no one wants to come, we could just go _____.

3) Circle the correct underlined words in this sentence so that it makes sense:
   Infact / In fact I have got alot /a lot to say thankyou / thank you for.

4) Circle the correct underlined words in each of these sentences so that they make sense:
   I really want my brother to get his driving license / licence so he can drive me to netball
   practise / practice. My advise / advice to him is to practise / practice as much as possible.

5) Circle the correct 'passed' or 'past' in these sentences:
   Judy has just passed / past her driving test. In the passed / past she took the bus.

6) Circle the correct 'affect' or 'effect' in each of these sentences:
   a) I hate the affect / effect sad films have on me.   b) This might affect / effect you.

7) Circle the correct 'accept' or 'except' in this sentence:
   Tom won't accept / except any criticism, accept / except from his brother.

8) Add 'where', 'were' and 'wear' correctly to these sentences:
   a) _____ are the doughnuts?   c) You're not allowed to _____ make-up at school.
   b) We _____ only joking.   d) I didn't know _____ we _____.

9) Rewrite the following sentences so that they make sense:
   a) The monkeys have taken there windscreen wipers.   c) Their so cute.
   b) They went over they're.

10) Circle the correct 'your' or 'you're' in these sentences:
    Your / You're a scruffy so-and-so. Just look at your / you're hair!

11) Circle the correct 'hear' or 'here' in these sentences:
    a) My gran can't hear / here very well.   b) I don't like it hear / here.

12) Rewrite these sentences so that they make sense:
    To chipmunks set off too the zoo. A squirrel shouted, "Can I come two?"

13) Rewrite the following sentences so that they make sense.
    a) Rahul isn't very through in his work.   c) Please go though to the kitchen.
    b) I like his clothes. I don't get his hairstyle thorough.

14) Circle the correct underlined words in this sentence so that it makes sense:
    I'm not sure whether /weather that peace /piece of cake will help Don lose / loose weight.

15) Add 'buy', 'by' or 'bye' correctly to this statement.
    I want to ____ a painting ____ a local artist, but he just can't say good____ to it.

16) Circle the correct underlined word in each of these sentences so that they make sense:
    a) Can you teach / learn me to dance?   b) I need to lend / borrow your cookery book.

17) Circle the correct underlined word in each of these sentences so that they make sense:
    a) Tilly brought / bought a new bike with her pocket money.
    b) Sorry Sir, I haven't brought / bought my P.E. kit today.

18) Circle the correct spellings:
    a) initial / inicial   c) caucious / cautious   e) strength / strenth   g) quest / qwest
    b) gest / guest   d) fiction / ficsion   f) tuff / tough   h) rythm / rhythm

Capital Letters

Using capital letters might seem pretty obvious, but it's worth starting with the basics...

Use capitals at the start of sentences

Every sentence has to start with a capital letter.

> The mouse built a rocket to get to the moon.

> His dog chased after him in an aeroplane.

It's made of cheese, you know.

Yeah and pigs can...

Good day old chaps!

Some words always start with a capital letter.

Some words start with a capital letter wherever they appear in a sentence:

1) People's names and titles: Romeo loved Juliet.   Prince Charming needs a haircut.

2) Names of companies: Bank of Jupiter   Bigfish Airways

> Names for particular people, places and things are called 'proper nouns' (see p.38).

3) Titles of books and plays: The Hobbit   Stig of the Dump

4) Towns and names of places: Narnia   Liverpool, Merseyside

5) Countries and nationalities: I am French. I come from France and I speak French.

6) Names of days and months: Saturday   23rd March

> 'I' is always written as a capital letter, no matter where it is in a sentence.

Capitalising some words can be tricky

There are some pesky nouns that are capitalised sometimes, but not at other times...

> Some queens like to eat cabbage.

> The Queen likes to eat cabbage.

If you're talking about queens in general, you don't need a capital letter.

If you're talking about a particular queen, you do need a capital letter.

The Queen of Narnia just loves capitals...

There we go then. A rundown of where and when you need to use capital letters — always at the start of a sentence, always with 'I', always with proper nouns and sometimes with other nouns.

Ending Sentences

Finishing a sentence in the right way helps make sure that the reader knows exactly what's going on. In fact, a sentence isn't a sentence without some lovely punctuation at the end.

Full stops end **sentences**

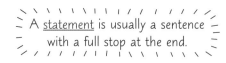

A statement is usually a sentence with a full stop at the end.

Full stops are dead easy — they go at the end of a sentence.

Trevor finished the race in 187th place.

Each sentence ends with a full stop.

His turtle was very proud of him.

In some sentences you replace the full stop with something else...

Question marks **show the end** *of a* **question**

Any sentence asking a question must end with a question mark instead of a full stop:

Would you like me to eat you?

Put a question mark here instead of a full stop.

Charlie asked the goldfish if it would like to be eaten.

The second sentence tells you about a question, but it doesn't ask one. So you don't need a question mark.

There's no question mark here.

Exclamation marks **show** *strong emotions*

This groovy symbol is an exclamation mark. You'll need one at the end of a sentence which shows a strong feeling:

Go away!

It was amazing!

Don't touch that cake!

Stop it!

You can use an exclamation mark:
1) if the sentence is a command.
2) for someone shouting.
3) to show a strong emotion.

You must only use one exclamation mark at a time.

I couldn't believe I was going to be on the Z Factor

NO! This makes your writing look like a barcode — and that's just silly.

I sentence you to using correct punctuation...

As a rule, the majority of your sentences should end with a nice simple full stop. But if you use a question or exclamation mark instead of a full stop, remember that you don't need both.

Commas

Commas are really important. They're <u>easy</u> to use, but <u>tricky</u> to <u>get right</u>, so pay attention.

Put commas between the items in a list

1) When you have a list, you <u>need</u> to put commas in. Here's why:

> I like roast chicken pizza ice cream and chips.

You don't want the <u>reader</u> to think that you're talking about ice cream which is '<u>roast chicken and pizza</u>' <u>flavoured</u>.

2) You use commas to <u>separate each thing</u> in the list:

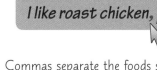

> I like roast chicken, pizza, ice cream and chips.

Commas separate the foods so you don't get them <u>mixed together</u>. You need to put '<u>and</u>' or '<u>or</u>' between the <u>last two</u> items in a list. You <u>don't need</u> to put a comma <u>before</u> the final '<u>and</u>' or '<u>or</u>'.

You only need to use <u>commas</u> in <u>lists</u> of <u>three or more</u> items.

3) You also need to use a <u>comma</u> to <u>separate</u> two <u>adjectives</u> when they are <u>describing different aspects</u> of something:

For more on <u>commas</u> and <u>adjectives</u> see p.46.

> He was a kind, wonderful aardvark.

Both these <u>adjectives</u> describe <u>different aspects</u> of the aardvark, so you <u>need</u> a <u>comma</u>.

Be careful when joining sentences with a comma

1) When you join two sentences with a <u>connective</u>, you sometimes need a <u>comma</u> as well.

2) Some <u>connectives</u> that usually need a comma are:

> <u>F</u>or, <u>A</u>nd, <u>N</u>or, <u>B</u>ut, <u>O</u>r, <u>Y</u>et & <u>S</u>o

or '<u>FANBOYS</u>'.

3) When one of these 'FANBOYS' is used to <u>join two sentences</u> together, the comma usually goes where the <u>next point begins</u>.

> The ice cream was tasty, but it made me ill.

> I love commas, so I use them in my work.

The <u>comma</u> and the <u>connective join</u> the two sentences.

4) <u>Longer linking words</u> — like '<u>however</u>' and '<u>nevertheless</u>' — are also <u>followed</u> by a <u>comma</u> when they appear at the <u>start</u> of a sentence.

See p.51 for more on <u>connectives</u>.

> However, the pizza was topped with chocolate sprinkles.

I comma-nd you to learn this page...

Thank goodness for <u>commas</u> — that ice cream sounded disgusting before the commas arrived. When you think you've taken in <u>everything</u> on this page, there are <u>more commas</u> coming up...

Commas

Here's another page about those <u>bearded full stops</u> that we call <u>commas</u>. Enjoy...

Commas separate *extra information*

1) You can use a <u>pair of commas</u> to separate extra information in the <u>middle</u> of a sentence:

> Mr Crystal, who lives next door, has just bought a tractor.

These commas <u>separate</u> the <u>extra bit</u> of information.

> The Tractor Racing Cup, which happens once a year, takes place in his field.

2) You can <u>check</u> you've used the commas <u>correctly</u> by removing the bit <u>inside</u> the commas. If the sentence <u>still makes sense</u>, then you've used them correctly:

> The tractor, which is red, can travel at 100 miles per hour.

This is the extra bit — if you <u>remove</u> it, the sentence should still make <u>sense</u>. Let's see...

> The tractor can travel at 100 miles per hour.

Excellent — the sentence does make <u>sense</u>, so the commas have been used <u>correctly</u>.

Don't stick commas *all over* the place

1) It's easy to go <u>comma crazy</u>, but make sure that you only put commas in the <u>right places</u>.

These two commas are <u>correct</u> — they separate the <u>extra information</u> about Mr Hunter.

> Mr Hunter, the organiser, said today, that the tournament would begin on 14th September.

The third comma is <u>wrong</u> — 'said today' and 'that the tournament...' go together — they're part of the <u>same</u> bit of information.

2) You should only use commas in lists, when you want to <u>join</u> <u>two sentences</u>, or when you want to add <u>extra information</u>. Randomly throwing in a bunch of commas just <u>doesn't work</u>.

Commas are for life — not just for Christmas...

Use them well, and commas will make your writing beautifully <u>clear</u> and <u>easy to understand</u>. Make sure that you don't put them in the <u>wrong places</u> though — otherwise there will be chaos.

Colons and Semicolons

Colons and semicolons are a bit trickier to use than commas, so read this page carefully.

Colons and semicolons are used for lists

1) You can use colons to introduce extra information — for example a list:

Bullet points can break up a list, so that each point stands out more.

To do list:
- mow the lawn
- do the washing
- cook dinner

2) You can use a semicolon to break up lists of long phrases or clauses. It's like using commas in a list except you need a semicolon before the last item.

> When I'm older, I want to go to the moon; play cricket against Martians, who are excellent at sports; and stay at a 17-star hotel, even though their prices are out of this world.

The last two things need a semicolon as well as the 'and' or 'or'.

They can also join sentences together

1) You can also use a colon to join two sentences when the second sentence explains something in the first sentence.

> Polar bears face a big problem: they are running out of soda.

The colon introduces an explanation. The bit after the colon doesn't need to be a full sentence.

2) Semicolons can also join two sentences. To use a semicolon you need two full sentences that are related, and both sentences must be equally important.

> Bruce likes dancing; Sheila likes surfing.

The semicolon joins these two sentences. The sentences are related, and they are of the same importance.

Colons and semicolons do different things

Colons and semicolons can affect the meaning of a sentence. A colon introduces explanation of the first sentence; a semicolon just links two sentences:

Tony

> Tony was delighted; Gordon was furious.

The semicolon shows that the two sentences are related but doesn't explain why Tony was delighted.

> Tony was delighted: Gordon was furious.

The colon shows the reader why Tony was delighted — it's because Gordon was furious.

This stuff really is a pain in the colon...
Don't be fooled by the similar names: colons and semicolons are used differently — get them right.

Brackets and Dashes

Learn how to use these chaps correctly and your writing will look great.

Put extra information in brackets

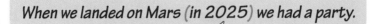
Brackets are also known as parentheses.

1) Brackets go around extra information in a sentence to keep it separate. If you take out the bit between the brackets, the sentence should still make sense.

> When we landed on Mars (in 2025) we had a party.

'In 2025' is the extra bit of information, so it goes inside the brackets.

2) You can also use them to separate an explanation or definition from the rest of the sentence.

> The M.A.T. (Martian Animal Trust) was founded in 2099.

The bit inside the brackets explains what the letters M.A.T. stand for.

3) If the information in brackets goes at the end of the sentence, the full stop goes outside the second bracket.

> Mars was too hot for my pet penguin (Beaky).

The full stop goes after the second bracket.

Dashes can do a similar thing

1) A pair of dashes can be used instead of brackets to add extra information:

> The farmers — Antonio and Josh — liked to eat cheese.

The extra info goes between the dashes.

dash

2) A single dash can give you a dramatic pause in a sentence:

> We thought Josh was normal — until we saw his feet.

DRAMATIC PAUSE! Think of it a bit like a drum roll in the middle of a sentence.

Don't dash past this page — it might come in useful...

Brackets and dashes are all about getting nice, natural pauses into your writing. For brackets, remember that the sentence must make sense without needing the bit inside the brackets. For dashes, make sure you know when to use one — and when to use two.

Hyphens

Hyphens may not be as cool as their big brother — the dash — but they're still important...

Hyphens join words or parts of words together

1) Hyphens can be used to join a prefix to a root word. You often need a hyphen when the prefix ends in the same letter that the root word begins with:

co-own   re-enter   semi-intelligent

> Flip to p.4 for some pointers on prefixes.

2) You can also use a hyphen when a word could be confused for another word.

I re-searched the Internet.   I researched the Internet.

This means: I searched the Internet again — e.g. looking for funny cat videos.

This means: I looked for information about the Internet — e.g. for a school project on... well, the Internet.

3) You need to use a hyphen if you're attaching a prefix to a root word which has a capital letter (e.g. a proper noun).

half-Scottish   post-Tudor   pro-French

Hyphens show which words go with which

1) Hyphens link words together to make the meaning clear.

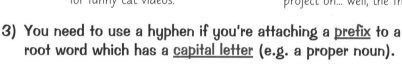

A man eating squid.   →   A man-eating squid.

Adding a hyphen changes the meaning...

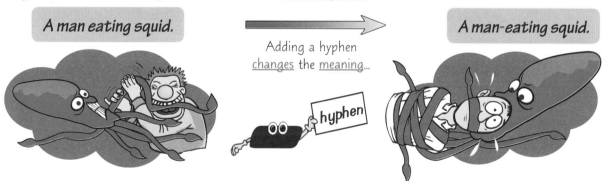

2) Here are some common examples of words and phrases that use hyphens:

vice-president   part-time   thirty-seven

middle-aged   mother-in-law   ex-girlfriend

> All written numbers between twenty-one and ninety-nine need hyphens.

Hyphens can be a lot of fun...

...but they're not much fun if you end up getting eaten by a squid. That poor man's experience should encourage you to put your hyphens in the right places — lives are at stake here, people...

Apostrophes and Missing Letters

The title of this page sounds a bit like some kind of crime novel... Sadly that's not what this page is about, but it'll be <u>useful</u> for you anyway. Time to <u>get reading</u>.

*Apostrophes **replace** missing letters*

Shortened words or phrases — like <u>haven't</u> and <u>don't</u> — use <u>apostrophes</u> to show where <u>letters</u> have been <u>removed</u>.

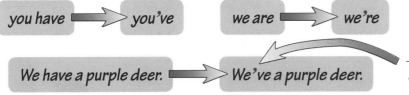

The <u>apostrophe</u> shows that the '<u>h</u>' and '<u>a</u>' of '<u>have</u>' are <u>missing</u>.

These forms *always* have an *apostrophe*

1) If you've got a phrase with <u>letters taken out</u>, you definitely need to use an <u>apostrophe</u>.

2) It's worth <u>learning</u> some of the most <u>common</u> ones:

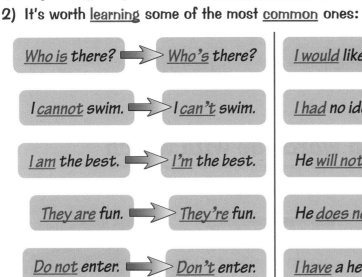

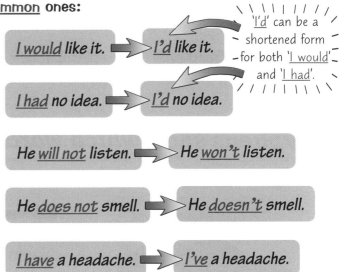

'<u>I'd</u>' can be a shortened form for both '<u>I would</u>' and '<u>I had</u>'.

*Let's **and** lets **mean** different things*

1) '<u>Let's</u>' is the shortened form of '<u>let us</u>'.

'<u>Let's</u>' needs an <u>apostrophe</u> here because the <u>shortened form</u> of '<u>let us</u>' is being used. The apostrophe shows the letter '<u>u</u>' is <u>missing</u>.

2) '<u>Lets</u>' means '<u>allows</u>' and doesn't need an apostrophe:

She <u>lets</u> him lick the spoon.

<u>No</u> apostrophe is needed here. 'Let us' <u>wouldn't</u> make sense.

Wanted: anyone with info about these missing letters...

This is quite simple really — if you <u>take out letters</u> to make a <u>shorter word</u>, you need to put an <u>apostrophe</u> in their place. Do that, and you can't go too far wrong. It's as easy as pie.

Possessive Apostrophes

My little brother's a bit like a <u>possessive apostrophe</u> — his sweets <u>belong to HIM</u>...

Use an apostrophe and '-s' to show ownership

1) <u>Add</u> an <u>apostrophe and '-s'</u> to show that something <u>belongs</u> to someone.

> The cat's whiskers glowed in the dark.

> The pear's skin was smooth.

The <u>apostrophe</u> and '<u>-s</u>' show that the whiskers <u>belong</u> to the cat, and the skin <u>belongs</u> to the pear.

2) If a word already <u>ends in 's'</u>, you should still <u>add an apostrophe and '-s'</u>. (Unless the word is <u>plural</u> — we'll cover that in a minute.)

> The hippopotamus's mud was delicious.

> Mrs Thomas's scones were disgusting.

You still <u>add</u> an '<u>-s</u>' to singular words <u>ending in</u> '<u>s</u>' to show <u>who owns what</u>.

Be careful with plurals and apostrophes

1) If the plural for a group of people or things <u>doesn't end in 's'</u>, like 'men' and 'women', you just add an <u>apostrophe</u> and '<u>-s</u>' to show <u>ownership</u>.

> I put the men's shoes in the toilet.

> Simon threw the women's shoes in the pond.

I guess they needed a wash...

2) If the plural for a group of people or things <u>does end in 's'</u>, then just stick an <u>apostrophe</u> on the <u>end of the word</u> (without adding another '-s').

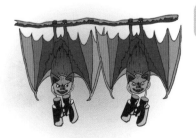

> I only saw the foxes' tails as they ran past me.

These words <u>already have</u> an '<u>s</u>' because they're <u>plural</u>, so they just need <u>the apostrophe</u>.

> The bats' binoculars were made by beetles.

The bat's binoculars — or the bats' binoculars...

Placing that little <u>apostrophe</u> can make a <u>big difference</u> to the <u>meaning</u> of a sentence. Putting one in the wrong place could mean that only one bat gets a pair of binoculars, and that would be sad.

It's and Its

Getting these two muddled up is one of the most common <u>grammatical mistakes</u> in the English language. So you can get one step ahead of the game by <u>learning</u> it <u>properly</u> now.

'It's' means 'it is' or 'it has'

1) If you write 'it's' with an <u>apostrophe</u>, you must <u>always</u> use it to mean '<u>it is</u>' or '<u>it has</u>'. The <u>apostrophe</u> shows that <u>letters</u> have been <u>missed out</u>.

<u>It is</u> raining today. ➡ <u>It's</u> raining today.

<u>It has</u> been a great year for ostriches. ➡ <u>It's</u> been a great year for ostriches.

2) The quickest way to <u>test</u> if you've used '<u>it's</u>' <u>correctly</u> is to replace 'it's' with '<u>it is</u>' or '<u>it has</u>'. Then see if the sentence still <u>makes sense</u>.

<u>It's</u> too cold to go fishing.

<u>It has</u> too cold to go fishing. ✗ — This <u>doesn't make sense</u>.

If <u>one</u> of them <u>fits</u>, the <u>apostrophe</u> is <u>correct</u>. **BUT**

<u>It is</u> too cold to go fishing. ✓ — This <u>makes sense</u>, so '<u>it's</u>' has been used <u>correctly</u>.

Its shows that something belongs to it

1) If there's <u>no apostrophe</u> then '<u>its</u>' shows something <u>belongs</u> to '<u>it</u>' (whatever 'it' is).

The whale flipped <u>its</u> tail.

The chipmunk opened <u>its</u> pack of nuts.

The tail <u>belongs</u> to the whale.

The nuts <u>belong</u> to the chipmunk.

2) You can do the <u>same test</u> by inserting '<u>it is</u>' or '<u>it has</u>' to check if you've used '<u>its</u>' correctly.

The ship lost <u>its</u> captain.

The ship lost <u>it has</u> captain. ✗ — This <u>doesn't make sense</u>.

If <u>neither</u> of them <u>fit</u>, '<u>its</u>' is <u>correct</u>.

The ship lost <u>it is</u> captain. ✗ — This <u>doesn't make sense</u> either, so '<u>its</u>' was <u>correct</u>.

Don't let 'its' (and 'it's') get you down...

I'm afraid that these are two words you simply <u>have to learn</u>, so that you can confidently use the right one each time. Remember, '<u>it's</u>' when it's short for '<u>it is</u>' or '<u>it has</u>', '<u>its</u>' for <u>possession</u>.

Inverted Commas

Inverted commas tell you when <u>someone is speaking</u>. Without them, things can get confusing.

Inverted commas *show when someone is speaking*

We go before the speech.

❝❝

Every time you're writing the <u>actual words</u> that someone <u>says</u> (<u>direct speech</u>), you need to use <u>inverted commas</u>.

We go after it.

❞ ❞

\ \ \ | | | / / /
\ Inverted /
~ commas can ~
- also be called -
/ <u>speech marks</u>. \
/ / / | | \ \ \

"Are you sure that this is the footpath?" asked Tim.

<u>Inverted commas</u> go at the <u>start</u> of speech...

... and at the <u>end</u>, to show that the person has <u>stopped talking</u>.

"Don't look down!" said the little man on the ground.

With <u>inverted commas</u>, it's clear what's <u>actually being said</u>.

I can't see Tim said.

At first it seems that someone <u>can't see Tim</u>.

"I can't see," Tim said.

This sentence <u>isn't clear</u> without inverted commas.

\ \ \ \ | | / / / / /
~ Flip over the page to see how ~
/ to <u>punctuate direct speech</u>. \
/ / | | | \ \ \

Not all speech needs *inverted commas*

1) If you're writing <u>about</u> what <u>someone said</u>, rather than <u>quoting</u> them <u>directly</u>, you <u>don't need</u> inverted commas. This is <u>reported speech</u>.

2) You only need inverted commas when you're writing someone's <u>actual words</u>.

Bill said that he wasn't afraid of the spider.

<u>No inverted commas</u> are needed here, because it's <u>reported speech</u>.

Get rid of it!

Bill said, "I'm not afraid of the spider."

This is <u>direct speech</u> (what Bill <u>actually said</u>), so we need <u>inverted commas</u>.

Marek said that he wanted to keep the spider as a pet, but Bill said, "I think we should take it outside."

This sentence has <u>both kinds</u> of speech. We <u>don't</u> know <u>Marek's actual words</u> — it's <u>reported speech</u> and <u>no inverted commas</u> are needed. We <u>do</u> know what <u>Bill actually said</u> — it's direct speech, so <u>inverted commas</u> are needed.

Mark my words — learn to use speech marks...

Inverted commas are nowhere near as scary as spiders, but you've still got to keep an eye out for them. Remember that when you're writing down someone's <u>actual words</u>, you need to put <u>inverted commas</u> around them to show that they're <u>speaking</u>. It makes everything much clearer.

Inverted Commas and Punctuation

Now you know about using <u>inverted commas</u>, there are a few rules to learn about how to <u>punctuate</u> <u>direct speech</u>. Don't worry if it seems tricky — our <u>revision questions</u> will help you <u>practise</u>.

Start with a capital letter

The <u>first word</u> that is spoken always <u>starts</u> with a <u>capital</u> <u>letter</u>, even if it <u>isn't</u> at the <u>beginning</u> of the <u>sentence</u>.

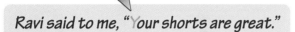

Ravi said to me, "Your shorts are great."

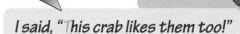

I said, "This crab likes them too!"

Speech always ends with a punctuation mark

It's important that you <u>end</u> speech properly. <u>Remember the rules</u> and you'll be golden:

1) If the sentence <u>ends</u> when the speech ends, put a <u>full stop</u> before the closing inverted commas.

2) If the sentence <u>continues</u> after the speech, put a <u>comma</u> before the closing inverted commas.

3) If the speech is a <u>command</u> or shows <u>strong feelings</u>, put an <u>exclamation mark</u> there instead.

4) If the speech is a <u>question</u>, put a <u>question mark</u> there.

Bob said, "It smells terrible."

This sentence has finished, so you need a <u>full stop</u>.

"I think it's stuck down there," Lenny added.

The speech has finished, but the sentence hasn't, so you need a <u>comma</u>.

Bob is shouting, so you need an <u>exclamation mark</u>.

"It smells!" yelled Bob

This is a question, so you need a <u>question mark</u>.

"How did you get in there?" he asked.

A final point: If the punctuation <u>doesn't belong</u> to the <u>speech</u>, it goes <u>outside</u> the <u>inverted commas</u>.

Did you hear him say, "I love skunks"?

The <u>question</u> isn't part of the <u>speech</u>, so the question mark shouldn't be part of it either.

Speech Marks — 10 out of 10 if you learn this page...

Like normal sentences, speech always <u>starts</u> with a <u>capital letter</u> and <u>ends</u> with a <u>punctuation mark</u> — and you already know all about <u>full stops</u>, <u>commas</u>, <u>exclamation marks</u> and <u>question marks</u>.

Revision Summary Questions

After all that you should know lots about punctuation — what it looks like, how it's used and where to use it. The best way to check whether you've learnt everything you need to is to have a go at these questions. You can flip back through this section for help if you need it.

1) Add capital letters to this sentence so that it's punctuated correctly:
on monday, i met a spanish man named javier at the beach.

2) Add capital letters, full stops and question marks to correctly punctuate these sentences:
a) i went to the zoo on friday   b) could i borrow some milk   c) the dog licked tim

3) Add commas to these sentences so that they are punctuated correctly:
a) Yesterday I saw pigs cows sheep and a giant turnip.
b) I bought a washing line three potatoes a calculator and twenty napkins.

4) Add commas to these sentences so that they are punctuated correctly:
a) Georgia enjoyed the film but Beth thought it was boring.
b) The dog needed a walk so Jill took her out on the fields.

5) Use commas to separate the extra information in these sentences:
a) Ian and Lesley our neighbours like to go on holiday to Greece.
b) Carol who loves movies has just made her own action film.

6) Divide up this passage using semicolons:
At the weekend Franz went skiing, swimming and horse riding he bought a hovercraft, a bouncy castle and a banjo and he prepared a three-course meal of soup, pasta and jelly.

7) Add a colon or a semicolon to these sentences so that they make sense:
a) The police need new helmets sandwiches no longer fit under their old ones.
b) Some people like a quiet life others are big risk-takers.

8) Use brackets to separate the extra information in these sentences:
a) Sadie's favourite meal is a roast dinner specifically roast beef.
b) The C.S.A.S. Coffee Shop Appreciation Society is a great place for coffee fans.

9) Put dashes into these sentences so that they are punctuated correctly:
a) I played squash every day until I broke my arm.   b) The winners Lee and Mark stood up.

10) Add hyphens to these sentences so that they are punctuated correctly:
a) The fire breathing dragon's father in law had just turned sixty six.
b) Luisa was the editor of a pro American magazine.

11) Replace the underlined words in these sentences with their shortened forms.
a) <u>I am</u> going out.   b) She <u>will not</u> like it.   c) <u>They are</u> too big.   d) <u>We have</u> arrived.

12) Circle the correct 'lets' or 'let's' in these sentences:
a) Joanne never lets / let's me win.   b) Lets / Let's have spaghetti tonight.

13) Circle the correct underlined word in these sentences:
a) The <u>mayors'</u> / <u>mayor's</u> wife was not impressed.
b) The <u>church's</u> / <u>churchs'</u> steeple is wonky.
c) Jacob watched as the <u>mens'</u> / <u>men's</u> bus drove off.
d) The <u>pupil's</u> / <u>pupils'</u> noses all turned blue.

14) Circle the correct 'its' or 'it's' in these sentences:
a) Its / It's time to go home.   b) Its / It's three o'clock.   c) The cat chased its / it's tail.

15) Correctly punctuate these sentences:
a) Brian asked what happens if I press this button   b) the world will end replied Nadeen

Nouns

Without <u>nouns</u>, none of us would have a <u>name</u>. There wouldn't even be a word for 'person'...

Nouns **are words for** *things*

1) <u>Common nouns</u> are words that name a <u>type</u> of <u>person</u> or <u>thing</u>.
There are loads of these, for example:

| hedgehog | balloon | nurse | window | woman | trumpet |

2) <u>Proper nouns</u> are the names of <u>particular people</u>, <u>places</u>,
<u>groups</u>, <u>months</u> and <u>days</u> of the <u>week</u> (amongst other things).

Proper nouns always start with a <u>capital</u> <u>letter</u> (see p.25).

October   June   New York

Greenfield United   Anna   Friday

3) A <u>collective noun</u> is a word for a <u>group of things</u>.

<u>flock</u> of sheep   <u>pack</u> of wolves   <u>bunch</u> of flowers

Not all nouns **are** *things* **you can** *touch*

<u>Abstract nouns</u> are things you can't <u>touch</u>, <u>see</u> or
<u>hear</u>, but <u>don't forget</u> them — they're still <u>nouns</u>:

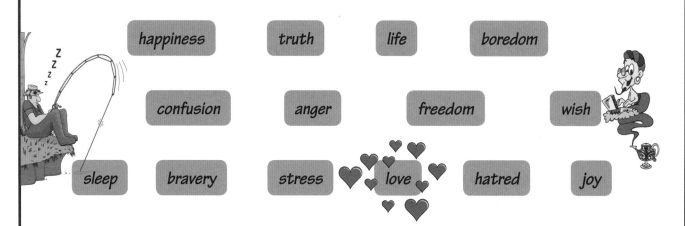

| happiness | truth | life | boredom |

| confusion | anger | freedom | wish |

| sleep | bravery | stress | love | hatred | joy |

A page of nouns — safer than a pack of wolves...

This is straightforward stuff, but there are some harder bits and bobs coming up, so make sure
you know this page <u>really well</u>. Watch out for those <u>proper nouns</u> — they always need a <u>capital</u>
<u>letter</u>, and don't forget about those sneaky <u>abstract nouns</u> — they might just catch you out.

Articles

'A', 'an' and 'the' — these three words only total six letters in all but they're still important...

Articles are 'a', 'an' and 'the'

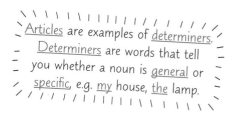

Articles are examples of determiners. Determiners are words that tell you whether a noun is general or specific, e.g. my house, the lamp.

1) Articles are the little words that go before nouns.

2) 'A' and 'an' are used for general things:

> Tim saw a film.   Katya went to a party.   Otto ate an orange.

These are all general things — it could be any film, any party or any orange.

an orange

an orange   an orange

3) 'The' is used for specific things:

> Tim saw the film.   Katya went to the party.   Otto ate the orange.

These are specific things — the sentences are talking about one particular film, orange or party.

the orange

You use 'an' and 'a' at different times

1) Use 'an' before a word beginning with a vowel (A, E, I, O or U).

> an accident   an insect   an umbrella

2) Use 'a' before a word beginning with a consonant (any letter that isn't a vowel).

> a tractor   a carrot   a scarecrow

3) Look out for exceptions that don't follow this rule.

> an honour   an hour   a unicorn   a European city

The 'h' is silent, so it sounds like these words begin with a vowel sound when you say them aloud. This means that they need 'an' rather than 'a'.

These words begin with vowels, but they sound like they begin with 'y' — a consonant sound, so you use 'a'.

'A' — easier to write than a newspaper article...

Remember, if the noun starts with a consonant sound you need 'a'. If it starts with a vowel sound you need 'an'. And if you're talking about a specific thing, you should always use 'the'.

Pronouns

Nope, 'pronoun' isn't short for 'professional noun' — in fact, their job is to replace nouns.

Pronouns take the place of nouns

You can use a pronoun to replace a noun so that you don't have to keep repeating it.

> Ian likes chess. Ian plays chess every day.

This is quite repetitive and boring. The nouns 'Ian' and 'chess' are both used twice.

This is much better. The pronouns 'he' and 'it' have replaced 'Ian' and 'chess'. This makes the sentences flow much better.

> Ian likes chess. He plays it every day.

These are the main pronouns

This rule is only for active sentences. Flip to p.70 for more on active and passive sentences.

There are two groups of pronouns — you use a different group depending on who in the sentence is doing the action.

| I | you | he | she | it | we | they |

These pronouns are used if the person or thing is doing the action.

> He found the treasure.   We sold the donkey.

These pronouns are used if the person (or thing) is having the action done to them (or it).

| me | you | him | her | it | us | them |

> The ball was thrown at him.   The donkey chased us.

These pronouns show possession

Possessive pronouns show you who or what owns something. Like the other pronouns, you use them to avoid having to repeat the same noun:

| mine | yours | his | hers | ours | theirs |

> That cow is ours.

'Ours' is a possessive pronoun — it shows who the cow belongs to.

> Alex needed a pencil, so Becca gave him hers.

The pronoun 'hers' replaces 'a pencil' in the second half of the sentence.

I hope those nouns don't mind being replaced...

Sentences are always better without repetition, sentences are always better without repetition, so pronouns are a handy way of making sure that you don't use the same noun again and again.

Pronouns

Seeing as that first page went so well, we've given <u>pronouns</u> a second chance to impress you...

Pronouns change for different numbers of people

1) <u>Pronouns change</u> depending on the <u>number of people</u> that you're talking about.

2) If you're talking about <u>one person or thing</u>, use a <u>singular pronoun</u>.
   If you're talking about <u>more than one person or thing</u>, use a <u>plural pronoun</u>. Simples.

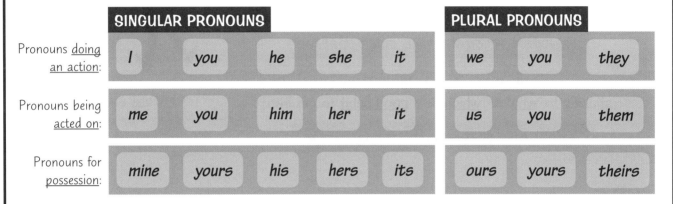

	SINGULAR PRONOUNS					PLURAL PRONOUNS		
Pronouns <u>doing an action</u>:	I	you	he	she	it	we	you	they
Pronouns being <u>acted on</u>:	me	you	him	her	it	us	you	them
Pronouns for <u>possession</u>:	mine	yours	his	hers	its	ours	yours	theirs

Make sure your pronouns are clear

1) You need to be <u>careful</u> that it's <u>clear</u> which noun each pronoun refers to.

    Sam went cycling with Phil and <u>he</u> didn't like it.

   It's <u>not clear</u> who didn't like cycling — it could be Sam or Phil.

2) Using <u>too many</u> pronouns might make things <u>confusing</u>.

   Alice thought <u>she</u> had spotted <u>her</u>, but <u>she</u> wasn't sure that <u>she</u> had.

   This sentence has <u>too many pronouns</u>. You can't work out what's <u>going on</u>.

Don't use 'me' when you mean 'I'

1) If a <u>pronoun</u> is <u>doing</u> the <u>action</u>, you need to use '<u>I</u>' not '<u>me</u>'.

   Don't forget — '<u>I</u>' is <u>always capitalised</u>.

   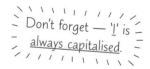 *Imran and <u>I</u> watched the match.*

   The '<u>I</u>' is <u>doing the action</u> (watching the match).

2) If you're not sure, <u>split</u> the sentence into <u>two</u> and test whether you <u>need</u> '<u>I</u>' or '<u>me</u>'.

   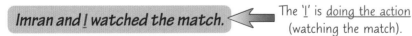 *Steph and <u>I</u> played golf.* → *Steph played golf.* ✓ / *<u>I</u> played golf.* ✓

   '<u>Me</u> played golf' <u>wouldn't make sense</u>, so '<u>I</u>' is <u>correct</u>.

Him and her and them and you and I — it's a date...

Things can get very <u>confusing</u> if pronouns aren't used <u>properly</u> — make sure it's clear <u>which person or thing</u> each pronoun refers to. It's OK to use the name of the noun sometimes too.

Who, Which and That

Three words coming up that you will simply use <u>all the time</u>, so it's definitely worth a <u>read</u>...

Use 'who' for people and 'which' or 'that' for things

1) Use '<u>who</u>' when you're talking about <u>people</u>:

> *Alf was the farmer <u>who</u> grew the giant carrot.*

2) Use '<u>which</u>' when you're talking about <u>animals</u> or <u>things</u>:

> *The carrot, <u>which</u> was huge, smelt of sheep.*

3) You can use '<u>that</u>' to refer to either <u>things or people</u>, but sticking to '<u>who</u>' or '<u>which</u>' is a <u>good habit</u> to get into:

> *I've got a car <u>that</u> is too big for my garage.*

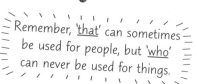

Remember, '<u>that</u>' can sometimes be used for people, but '<u>who</u>' can never be used for things.

There are two ways to use 'who', 'which' & 'that'

1) You can use '<u>who</u>' and '<u>which</u>' when you ask a <u>question</u>:

> *<u>Who</u> left their polar bear outside the cinema?*

> *<u>Which</u> cinema did you go to?*

If you use '<u>which</u>' to ask a question, there needs to be a <u>limited number</u> of <u>possible answers</u>. Otherwise you need to use '<u>what</u>'.

2) You can also use 'who', 'which' and 'that' to <u>link two sentences</u> together:

> If you're talking about <u>people</u>, use '<u>who</u>' or '<u>that</u>':
>
> *Henry VIII was an English king.*   *He had six wives.*
>
> *Henry VIII was an English king <u>who</u> had six wives.*

'Who' and 'that' can <u>join</u> the <u>two sentences together</u> by <u>replacing</u> the <u>pronoun</u> at the start of the second sentence.

> If you're talking about <u>things</u>, use '<u>which</u>' or '<u>that</u>':
>
> *I bought some beans.*   *They turned out to be magical.*
>
> *I bought some beans <u>which</u> turned out to be magical.*

'Which' <u>replaces</u> the <u>pronoun</u> 'they' when it <u>joins</u> the <u>two sentences together</u>.

3) When you use a <u>relative pronoun</u> like 'who' or 'which' to <u>join two clauses</u>, the subordinate clause is known as a <u>relative clause</u>. See p.50 for more on subordinate clauses.

Grab your cat and broomstick for some which-craft...

'<u>Who</u>' and '<u>which</u>' are easy to remember — '<u>who</u>' is only used for <u>people</u>, and '<u>which</u>' is only used with <u>things</u>. '<u>That</u>' is less fussy — it can be used with <u>either people or things</u>. Get learning...

Who, Whom and Whose

'<u>Who</u>' and '<u>whom</u>' are quite tricky to get your head round, but practice makes perfect...

'Who' and 'whom' are tricky

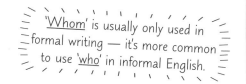

'<u>Whom</u>' is usually only used in formal writing — it's more common to use '<u>who</u>' in informal English.

1) If the <u>thing</u> you're talking about is the <u>subject</u> of a sentence — <u>doing the action</u> — use '<u>who</u>'.

2) You use '<u>whom</u>' with the <u>object</u> of a sentence — the <u>thing</u> having the <u>action done to it</u>.

> *Mo is the lady <u>who</u> does the teas.*

Mo is the <u>subject</u>, so you need 'who'.

> *<u>Whom</u> did she invite?*

'<u>She</u>' is the <u>subject</u> and '<u>whom</u>' is the <u>object</u>.

3) If you're not sure, try replacing 'who' or 'whom' with '<u>he</u>', '<u>she</u>' or '<u>they</u>'. If the sentence still <u>makes sense</u>, use '<u>who</u>'. If it <u>doesn't</u>, use '<u>whom</u>'.

> *<u>Mo</u> does the teas.* ➡ *<u>She</u> does the teas.* ✓

> *<u>Whom</u> did she invite?* ➡ *Did she invite <u>whom</u>?* ➡ *Did she invite <u>they</u>?* ✗

You might need to <u>rearrange</u> the <u>sentence</u> to do this test.

This sentence should be 'Did she invite <u>them</u>?' — '<u>whom</u>' is <u>correct</u>.

4) If this is a bit tricky, stick to using '<u>who</u>' in <u>informal writing</u>, and only use '<u>whom</u>' <u>after</u> a <u>preposition</u> in <u>formal writing</u>. It's not <u>foolproof</u>, but you'll get it <u>right</u> most of the time.

> *<u>From whom</u> did you get your lunch?*

'<u>From</u>' is a <u>preposition</u> (see p.51), so you use '<u>whom</u>' instead of '<u>who</u>'.

> *To <u>whom</u> it may concern,*

This would be used in a <u>formal letter</u> if you didn't know the person you were writing to.

'Who's' means 'who is', but 'whose' is possessive

1) '<u>Who's</u>' is the <u>shortened</u> form of '<u>who is</u>' or '<u>who has</u>'.

> *<u>Who's</u> going to watch the fireworks?*

This means, '<u>Who is</u> going to watch the fireworks?'

2) '<u>Whose</u>' is a way of saying '<u>belonging to whom</u>'.

> *<u>Whose</u> book is this?*

> *The police couldn't decide <u>whose</u> dog was to blame.*

This means 'to whom does this book belong?'

You can <u>test</u> you've used '<u>whose</u>' <u>correctly</u> by <u>replacing</u> it with '<u>who is</u>' or '<u>who has</u>'. In this sentence, neither of those make sense, so '<u>whose</u>' is <u>correct</u>.

Who's bothered about who, whom and whose...?

Well <u>you</u> definitely should be. '<u>Who's</u>' and '<u>whose</u>' are easy to <u>test</u> to see if you've used them correctly — just replace them with '<u>who is</u>' or '<u>who has</u>' and see if the sentence still <u>makes sense</u>.

Verbs

Verbs tell you what is going on in a sentence — that makes them pretty important then...

There are *two main types* of verbs:

1) Doing words

Remember that every sentence has to have at least one verb in it, otherwise it's not a sentence (see p.48).

Doing words like 'run' and 'jump' are a type of verb that describes an action — they tell you what is happening in a sentence.

> kick   wish   jump   eat   throw   shout

> Jacob plays the drums.   Karl dances every day.

2) Being words

1) Being words are the other type of verb — they tell you how something is.

2) All of the being words come from the verb 'to be'.

> am   is   were   are   was

> I am sporty.   Tomas is on holiday.

The girls are behind the sofa.

Verbs *need something to do the* action

1) Verbs need a noun (or pronoun) to do the action. In most sentences, the thing doing the action comes just before the verb.

> Gwen made a cake.

This is an active sentence. The focus is on 'Gwen', the subject who is doing the action.

2) Passive sentences (see p.70) are a bit different — it won't be so clear which noun goes with the verb, but in most cases you still need something to do the action, otherwise the sentence won't make sense.

> The cake was made by Gwen.

This is a passive sentence. The focus is on 'the cake' — 'Gwen' is no longer the subject, but she is still doing the action.

I like verbs — they taste great in soup...

Don't forget about those being words — they're verbs too — it's not just about the doing words. And don't leave those verbs on their own — someone or something needs to do the action.

Verbs

Hopefully you now get <u>what</u> verbs are, so it's time to make sure you're using them <u>properly</u>.

Verbs **must agree** *with whoever is doing them*

1) Verbs need to 'agree' with their <u>subject</u> — the person or thing <u>doing the action</u>.

2) This means that if the <u>person</u> doing the action is <u>singular</u>, the <u>verb</u> has to be <u>singular</u> too.

The <u>frog lives</u> in the pond. ← '<u>The frog</u>' is the <u>subject</u> — it's doing the living. 'Frog' is <u>singular</u>, so the <u>verb</u> (to live) must also be <u>singular</u> — 'lives'.

'<u>The frogs</u>' are the <u>subject</u> in this sentence. 'Frogs' is <u>plural</u>, so the <u>verb</u> must be <u>plural</u> — 'live'. → *The <u>frogs live</u> in the pond.*

 *<u>Richard and Kat sweep</u> the floor every day.*   *<u>Gerald sweeps</u> the floor every day.*

There are <u>two people</u> doing the sweeping, so the <u>verb</u> must be <u>plural</u> — 'sweep'.

There's just <u>one person</u> doing the sweeping in this sentence, so the <u>verb</u> must be <u>singular</u> — 'sweeps'.

Raj <u>swims</u> in the lake. → *Raj and I <u>swim</u> in the lake.*

This <u>wouldn't make sense</u> if it said 'Raj swim in the lake.'

As the <u>subject</u> becomes <u>plural</u>, the <u>verb</u> becomes <u>plural</u> to <u>agree</u>.

Verbs help show **when something is** happening

1) <u>Verbs</u> also <u>change</u> depending on <u>when</u> the action is taking place. These different verb forms are called <u>tenses</u>.

> There's a whole section on <u>tenses</u> coming up on p.58.

2) Verbs can be in the <u>present tense</u>, the <u>past tense</u> or the <u>future tense</u>.

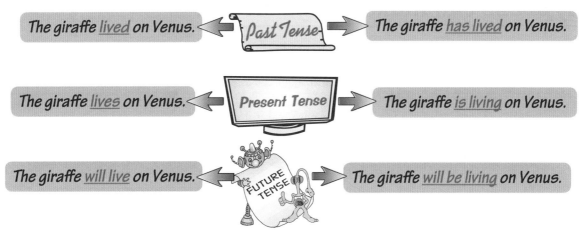

The giraffe <u>lived</u> on Venus. ← Past Tense → *The giraffe <u>has lived</u> on Venus.*

The giraffe <u>lives</u> on Venus. ← Present Tense → *The giraffe <u>is living</u> on Venus.*

The giraffe <u>will live</u> on Venus. ← FUTURE TENSE → *The giraffe <u>will be living</u> on Venus.*

I wonder if the Queen agrees with her subjects...

OK then, the main thing to remember is that <u>verbs change</u> to <u>agree</u> with their <u>subject</u> — having a <u>plural verb</u> with a <u>singular subject</u> wouldn't make sense. So get it right...

Adjectives

Adjectives bring a bit of <u>colour</u> to the party — they'll make your writing lovely and descriptive.

Adjectives modify nouns

1) <u>Adjectives</u> tell you <u>more</u> about <u>nouns</u> by adding <u>specific details</u>.

2) They tell you how something <u>looks</u> or <u>feels</u>.

OK, I lied about the flower. Sorry.

> The <u>brown</u> dog barked.

The <u>adjective</u> tells you about the <u>colour</u> of the dog.

> I was very <u>nervous</u>.

'Nervous' is an <u>adjective</u>. It describes the <u>feelings</u> of the noun — 'I'.

> The flower was <u>massive</u>.

'Massive' describes the <u>size</u> of the flower.

Sometimes you'll need commas between adjectives

1) If you use <u>more than one adjective</u> to describe something you might need to use <u>commas</u> to separate them.

> There are <u>serious</u>, <u>blue</u>, <u>tall</u> men in my house.

These <u>adjectives</u> all describe <u>different aspects</u> of the men. This means they are a <u>list of adjectives</u>, so they need <u>commas</u> between them.

2) If you've used <u>more than one</u> adjective to describe the <u>same aspect</u> of the noun, you <u>don't need</u> a <u>comma</u>:

> Abe had a <u>pale blue</u> jacket.

'<u>Pale</u>' and '<u>blue</u>' are both adjectives, but they don't need a comma because they <u>both describe</u> the <u>colour</u> of the jacket.

> They had <u>Chinese silk</u> bow ties.

'<u>Chinese</u>' and '<u>silk</u>' are both <u>adjectives</u> describing the <u>material</u> of the bow ties. This means you <u>don't need</u> a <u>comma</u>.

Hyphens can make things clearer

For more examples of <u>hyphens</u> in action, flick back to p.31.

Sometimes you might have to use a <u>hyphen</u> when you use <u>more</u> than <u>one adjective</u>:

> He had a high tech job.

At first glance '<u>high</u>' could refer to the job being <u>high up</u> in the business. But a <u>hyphen</u> makes it <u>clearer</u>...

> He had a high-tech job.

> There were fifty one day passes.

<u>Numbers</u> can sometimes be <u>adjectives</u>. Adding a <u>hyphen</u> makes the meaning <u>clearer</u>.

> There were fifty one-day passes.

> There were fifty-one day passes.

Adjectives — making nouns prettier since 1791...

Life without <u>adjectives</u> would be very boring — everything would be in black and white for a start. <u>Learn</u> this page so that you know exactly when to include <u>commas</u> and <u>hyphens</u> too.

Adverbs

It's easy to remember what an <u>adverb</u> does — it <u>adds information</u> about a <u>verb</u>.

Adverbs describe verbs

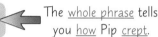
Adding the <u>suffix</u> '<u>-ly</u>' to an <u>adjective</u> usually makes it into an <u>adverb</u> — e.g. 'quick' becomes '<u>quickly</u>'.

1) <u>Adverbs</u> tell you <u>how</u> or <u>when</u> an action was done. Most adverbs <u>end</u> in '<u>-ly</u>'.

> *Christina knits <u>quickly</u>.*

> *Emily <u>suddenly</u> appeared.*

> *Pip came home <u>late</u>.*

The adverb <u>describes the verb</u> — it tells you that the knitting was done quickly.

Adverbs can also come <u>before the verb</u> — it still describes how the verb was done.

Watch out for adverbs that don't <u>end in '-ly'</u>.

2) Adverbs can also be a <u>group of words</u> — an <u>adverbial phrase</u>.

> *Pip crept through the house <u>as quietly as a mouse</u>.*

The <u>whole phrase</u> tells you <u>how</u> Pip <u>crept</u>.

3) You can also <u>describe adjectives</u> using an adverb. Words like '<u>really</u>', '<u>quite</u>' and '<u>very</u>' are all <u>adverbs</u>. They show <u>how much</u> an <u>adjective modifies</u> a <u>noun</u>.

> *a <u>very</u> happy dog*

The <u>adverb</u> describes how happy the dog is.

4) Finally, an adverb can <u>describe another adverb</u>.

> *Liam runs <u>really quickly</u>.*

The <u>main adverb</u> is 'quickly' — it describes the 'running'. The <u>second adverb</u> is 'really', which tells you <u>more about how</u> 'quickly' it was.

Don't confuse adjectives and adverbs

1) Some tricky words that end in '<u>-ly</u>' are <u>adjectives</u> and <u>not adverbs</u>.

> *Heather is a <u>friendly</u> girl.*

'Friendly' is usually an <u>adjective</u>, not an adverb. In this sentence, it describes the noun — 'girl'.

Some other <u>adjectives</u> <u>ending</u> in '<u>-ly</u>' to watch out for are: ugly, lonely, lovely and unlikely.

2) To <u>check</u> if a word is an <u>adjective</u> or an adverb, work out whether it is <u>describing</u> the <u>noun</u> or not.

> *<u>Most</u> people like chips.*

'Most' is an <u>adjective</u> <u>describing</u> the noun 'people'.

> *It was a <u>most</u> interesting lesson.*

'Most' is an <u>adverb</u> in this sentence. It <u>adds more information</u> to the <u>adjective</u> 'interesting'.

"Doctor, I feel like an adverb." "Don't ly to me..."

Adverbs <u>add detail</u> to a <u>verb or adjective</u>. If a word ends in '<u>-ly</u>', then ask what that word is describing. If it's describing a <u>verb</u> it's an <u>adverb</u>, but if it's <u>describing</u> a <u>noun</u> it's an <u>adjective</u>.

Sentence Structure

Everyone loves a <u>tasty sentence</u> — follow this <u>recipe</u> for yours and you <u>won't go far wrong</u>.

Sentences *must contain a complete idea*

1) Most of what you write needs to be in <u>proper sentences</u>.
   Every sentence must <u>contain a complete idea</u>.

2) If you <u>can't understand</u> what a sentence is supposed
   to be <u>about</u>, then it's probably <u>not a proper sentence</u>.

Sentences *need a* verb

1) A sentence has to be <u>about something</u> for it to <u>make sense</u>.

2) This means it has to have a <u>verb</u> or <u>nothing can happen</u> at all.

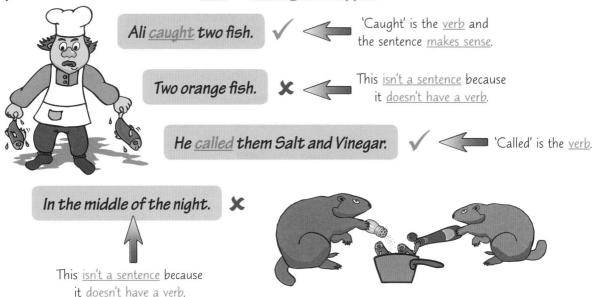

Ali <u>caught</u> two fish. ✓   'Caught' is the <u>verb</u> and the sentence <u>makes sense</u>.

Two orange fish. ✗   This <u>isn't a sentence</u> because it <u>doesn't have a verb</u>.

He <u>called</u> them Salt and Vinegar. ✓   'Called' is the <u>verb</u>.

In the middle of the night. ✗

This <u>isn't a sentence</u> because it <u>doesn't have a verb</u>.

Sentences *must make a clear point*

You should <u>decide</u> what you want to say <u>before</u> writing any sentence.
Otherwise you'll end up with sentences that <u>don't make any sense</u>.

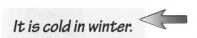

It is cold in winter.   A sentence can be very short if it <u>makes sense</u>, has a <u>verb</u> and has a clear point — winter is cold.

Have a quick think <u>before you write</u> a sentence to make sure that your <u>reader</u> is going to <u>understand</u> what's going on.   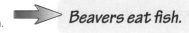 *Beavers eat fish.*

Verbs — *this season's 'must-have' for all sentences...*

<u>Sentences</u> come in all shapes and sizes, but what they all have in common is that they <u>make sense</u> on their own, they contain at least one <u>verb</u>, and they make a <u>clear point</u>.

Phrases and Clauses

I'm not going to lie — this stuff can be <u>tricky</u>, but if you <u>read it carefully</u> it'll soon make sense.

Sentences are made up of clauses and phrases

1) A <u>clause</u> is a part of a sentence which has a <u>subject</u> and a <u>verb</u>.
It <u>usually makes sense on its own</u> and some clauses can be used as a <u>separate sentence</u>.

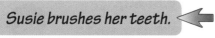 *Susie brushes her teeth.* ← This is a <u>clause</u> — it's got a <u>subject</u>, 'Susie', and a <u>verb</u>, 'brushes'. It makes sense as a sentence <u>on its own</u>.

2) A <u>phrase</u> is another part of a sentence, which <u>either</u> doesn't have a verb, <u>or</u> doesn't have a subject (some phrases might have <u>neither</u>).

'At the pond' is a <u>phrase</u> — it <u>doesn't have</u> a <u>subject</u> or a <u>verb</u>, and it <u>isn't a full sentence</u>. → 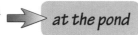 *at the pond*

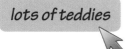 *lots of teddies*   *lots of soft, cuddly teddies with fuzzy fur*

These are <u>noun phrases</u>. A noun phrase is a phrase which acts as a <u>single noun</u>. In both these examples, the noun is simply '<u>teddies</u>'.

Phrases and clauses add information to sentences

1) Phrases and clauses <u>describe</u> things — they do a similar job to <u>adjectives</u> and <u>adverbs</u> (see p.46-47).

2) You can <u>add</u> them to sentences to add <u>extra information</u>.

Gary watches television. ← This is a <u>clause</u>. It's a <u>simple sentence</u>.

'When he gets home' is another <u>clause</u>. It acts like an <u>adverb</u> — it's telling you <u>when</u> Gary watches television. → *Gary watches television <u>when he gets home</u>.*

Gary watches television <u>with a cap on</u>. ← 'With a cap on' is a <u>phrase</u>. It <u>doesn't</u> have a <u>verb</u> and <u>doesn't make sense</u> on its own. It <u>adds information</u> about <u>how</u> Gary watches television.

 *In the morning,*   *Gary writes letters*   *at his desk.*

This is an '<u>adverbial phrase</u>'. It doesn't have a <u>verb</u>, so it's a <u>phrase</u>. It tells you <u>when</u> Gary writes.

This is a <u>clause</u> — it has a <u>verb</u> and a <u>subject</u>.

This is also a <u>phrase</u>. It gives you extra <u>information</u> about <u>where</u> Gary writes.

Clauses — not to be confused with a group of Santas...

<u>Phrases and clauses</u> are basically just <u>groups of words</u> that make up <u>sentences</u>. If you can remember that <u>clauses</u> always need a <u>verb and a subject</u>, then you should be fine this Christmas.

Clauses

Compound and complex sentences sound a bit scary, but they're not too hard. Here we go...

*Two main clauses **make up a** compound sentence*

1) A main clause is a clause that makes sense as a separate sentence.

2) A compound sentence is a sentence made of two main clauses which are equally important.

3) You join two main clauses using conjunctions (see p.51-52).

You have to use one of the 'FANBOYS' (for, and, nor, but, or, yet, so) to make compound sentences.

Dani likes lamb.   *Ellie is a vegetarian.*

To join these two main clauses you need to add a conjunction.

Dani likes lamb, | *but* | *Ellie is a vegetarian.*

The conjunction, 'but', makes this a compound sentence. It has two main clauses of equal importance that are joined by a conjunction.

*Complex sentences **have subordinate** clauses*

1) A complex sentence has a main clause and a less important clause.

2) The less important clause is called a subordinate clause. Subordinate clauses usually start with conjunctions like 'while', 'until', or 'because' (or any other conjunction that isn't one of the 'FANBOYS').

Dani ate lamb for dinner | *while Ellie was out.*

Main Clause   Conjunction   'while Ellie was out' is a subordinate clause

*Subordinate clauses **don't** make sense **alone***

You can tell main clauses and subordinate clauses apart because main clauses make sense on their own — subordinate clauses don't.

You only include a conjunction as part of a clause if it is NOT one of the FANBOYS.

I'm going to go canoeing until it goes dark.

'I'm going to go canoeing' is a main clause — it makes sense on its own.

'Until it goes dark' is a subordinate clause — it doesn't make sense on its own.

Sometimes the subordinate clause comes before the main clause.

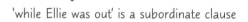
Because it's so dark, I'm going to light a fire.

The main clause makes sense without the subordinate clause.

Cats — experts at all sorts of clauses...

Subordinate clauses don't make sense on their own, and they join with a main clause to form complex sentences. Compound sentences need two main clauses and a conjunction.

Prepositions and Conjunctions

Feeling prepared for a page on <u>prepositions</u> and <u>conjunctions</u>? Off you go then...

Prepositions give information about where & when

1) Some <u>prepositions</u> tell you <u>where</u> things are <u>in relation to other things</u> in a sentence.

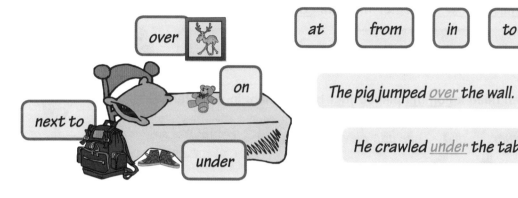

at | from | in | to | through

The pig jumped <u>over</u> the wall.

He crawled <u>under</u> the table.

2) Other prepositions tell you <u>when</u> things happen in <u>relation to each other</u>.

Some <u>prepositions</u> can act as <u>conjunctions</u>, e.g. <u>before</u>.

Let's go inside <u>before</u> it snows.

Lots of people go abroad <u>during</u> the summer.

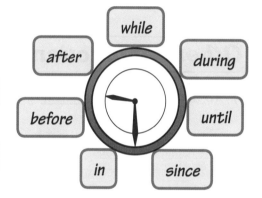

while | after | during | before | until | in | since

Conjunctions join bits of a sentence together

Conjunctions <u>join clauses</u> together to make a <u>longer sentence</u>. They usually go <u>in between</u> the <u>two clauses</u>.

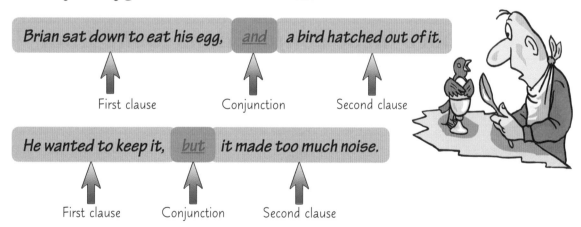

Brian sat down to eat his egg, | and | a bird hatched out of it.

First clause | Conjunction | Second clause

He wanted to keep it, | but | it made too much noise.

First clause | Conjunction | Second clause

Prepositions — not just places arranged beforehand...

<u>Conjunctions</u> and <u>prepositions</u> are <u>handy little words</u> that can usually be found in the middle of sentences, <u>linking clauses</u> together or <u>adding information</u>. And they can do even more <u>incredible things</u>, which you'll learn about on the next page. But for now, have a quick <u>break</u> and a <u>biscuit</u>.

Conjunctions

This page follows the <u>previous three</u> perfectly, so give them a <u>quick read</u> if you haven't already.

Use *FANBOYS* to make *compound sentences*

1) The word '<u>FANBOYS</u>' is a great way of <u>remembering</u> the list of <u>conjunctions</u> that can <u>join main clauses</u> together to make <u>compound sentences</u>.

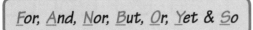 

For, *And*, *Nor*, *But*, *Or*, *Yet* & *So* ➡ FANBOYS

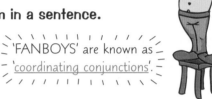

2) <u>FANBOYS</u> often need a <u>comma</u> placed <u>just before</u> them in a sentence.

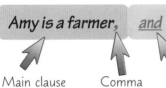

Amy is a farmer,   *and*   *she has eleven turkeys.*

'FANBOYS' are known as '<u>coordinating conjunctions</u>'.

Main clause   Comma   Conjunction   Main clause

Other conjunctions *make* complex sentences

1) To make <u>complex sentences</u> you need to use a <u>conjunction</u> that isn't one of the **FANBOYS**.

These are examples of '<u>subordinating conjunctions</u>'.

| *if* | *although* | *while* | *because* | *since* |

2) These conjunctions <u>join subordinate clauses</u> to <u>main clauses</u> and usually <u>don't need a comma</u>.

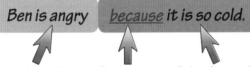 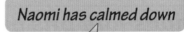

Ben is angry   *<u>because</u> it is so cold.*   *Naomi has calmed down*   *<u>since</u> he arrived.*

Main clause   Conjunction   Subordinate clause   Main clause   Conjunction   Subordinate clause

You can move *these* conjunctions *to the* front

1) A <u>subordinating conjunction</u> and its <u>connected clause</u> can be used at the <u>start of a sentence</u>.

2) If you want to write a sentence like this, you do <u>need a comma</u> after the subordinate clause.

<u>Because</u> it's so cold,   *Ben is angry.*   *<u>If</u> it snows,*   *Ben will stay in bed.*

The <u>conjunction</u>, 'because', and the rest of the <u>subordinate clause</u>, 'it's so cold', are <u>followed</u> by a <u>comma</u> and then the <u>main clause</u>.

You <u>always</u> need a <u>comma</u> when a <u>subordinate clause</u> comes at the <u>start</u> of a <u>sentence</u>.

FANBOYS — perfect for a hot day, or a bit of grammar...

These <u>conjunctions</u> may seem like <u>small words</u>, but they make a <u>big difference</u> in sentences — especially if you want to write <u>longer ones</u>. Don't forget when to use commas though...

Paragraphs

Paragraphs are important for making sure that your writing is presented well and easy to read.

Paragraphs make your writing clearer

Paragraphs break up big chunks of text, so that it's much easier to read.

I must break up the text.

The paragraphs space out the text and make it easier to read.

> The monster was prowling through the streets when suddenly it smelt food. The smell was coming from the house at the end of the road. The monster approached the front door in the light of the full moon. There was a crash and Henry sat up in bed. He listened carefully, but the whole house was quiet. Nothing stirred in the darkness, and as Henry listened, he could hear the pounding of his own heartbeat. Downstairs, the monster started to explore. It followed its nose towards the fridge. The smell was coming from the pie Henry's mum had made. The monster gobbled it up.

Long blocks of text are difficult to read.

> The monster was prowling through the streets when suddenly it smelt food. The smell was coming from the house at the end of the road. The monster approached the front door in the light of the full moon.
>
> There was a crash and Henry sat up in bed. He listened carefully, but the whole house was quiet. Nothing stirred in the darkness, and as Henry listened, he could hear the pounding of his own heartbeat.
>
> Downstairs, the monster started to explore. It followed its nose towards the fridge. The smell was coming from the pie Henry's mum had made. The monster gobbled it up.

Make the beginning and the end clear

1) You need to lay paragraphs out correctly:

2) Leave a gap before you write the first word of each paragraph.

3) At the end of each paragraph, put a full stop and then leave the rest of that line blank.

> Llamas are wonderful animals, but they can't use paragraphs. They don't know that you need to end each paragraph with a full stop.
>
> They often forget that you need to start each paragraph with a gap at the front.

Leave a gap before the first word.

Leave the rest of the line blank.

Use double strikes to show new paragraphs

If you forget to start a new paragraph, you can use a double strike ('//') to show the reader where the new paragraph should have started.

A double strike shows where the new paragraph should have begun.

> Llamas have been given old reading glasses so that they can begin writing lessons. They are all very excited about this opportunity. // Farmers hope that educating their llamas will lead to increased wool production.

Double strikes — paragraphs are good at bowling...

Hopefully you should now be quite confident about how to set out paragraphs — the next page will tell you all about when to use them in your work. Sadly there won't be any more llamas.

Paragraphs

Settle down, settle down, contain your <u>excitement</u> — it's a second page of <u>paragraphs</u>...

Start a new paragraph for each new point...

A new paragraph can show that you're making a <u>different point</u>.

This is a <u>new point</u>, so it needs a <u>new paragraph</u>.

> For centuries the inhabitants of Lemonville have produced some of the finest sherbet lemons in the world. This year they hope to win the Confectionery Championships for a record twentieth time.
>
> Another town hoping for sweet success will be Limecastle, whose legendary chocolate limes have recently been given a radical makeover.

...or when you write about something different

1) You need a new paragraph every time <u>something changes</u>.
2) This could be:

A <u>new character</u> appearing.

<u>Someone</u> different <u>speaking</u>.

A <u>different time</u>.

A <u>new place</u>.

<u>Time</u> has moved on.

Someone has started to <u>speak</u>.

Someone else has started to <u>speak</u>.

This is a <u>different place</u>.

> Chris was bored. The television was broken, the Internet was down and even the cat had disappeared.
>
> After a while, the phone rang and Chris ran into the kitchen to answer it. It was Nasreen.
>
> "Hi, Chris! Are you busy?" she asked. "Something incredible is happening outside — you should come round and have a look," she said, clearly very excited.
>
> "What's happening, Naz?" Chris was bored, but he didn't want to go out in the rain unless it was something really worth seeing. Nasreen had already put the phone down, so Chris had to take a chance and go and see for himself.
>
> When he got to Nasreen's house, he couldn't believe his eyes — the whole front garden was covered in frogs.

Graphs everywhere and this isn't even a maths book...

Basically, if you want to write about <u>something different</u>, introduce a <u>different character</u>, or talk about a <u>new time or place</u>, you need to use a <u>new paragraph</u>. Mind the frogs now...

Negatives

Chances are that you'll need to use <u>negatives</u> at some point, so <u>don't miss</u> this page out...

You can only use one type of negative at a time

1) If you use a <u>negative</u> in a sentence, make sure you only use <u>one at a time</u>.

2) A <u>double negative</u> is when you have <u>two</u> 'nos' or 'nots' in a sentence.
Two negatives cancel each other out — it means the sentence <u>won't make sense</u>.

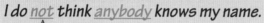 *I do <u>not</u> think <u>anybody</u> knows my name.* ✓

This is <u>correct</u> as there is only <u>one</u> negative — '<u>not</u>' — 'I do not think...'

'I do <u>not</u> think <u>no</u>body knows my name' would be <u>wrong</u> — it'd be a <u>double negative</u> and wouldn't make sense.

 There's <u>no</u> way he's <u>not</u> coming. ✗

This sentence is <u>incorrect</u> as there are <u>two negatives</u> — '<u>no</u>' and '<u>not</u>'.

This should say 'He's definitely coming'. Even if the sentence sort of makes sense, you should <u>never</u> use a <u>double negative</u>.

3) Avoid using the word '<u>no</u>' in phrases with '<u>-n't</u>' or '<u>not</u>'. You should use '<u>any</u>' instead.

 Basil ca<u>n't</u> find <u>any</u> trousers. ✓

'Ca<u>n't</u>' is the <u>only negative</u> in this sentence, so this is correct.

'Basil ca<u>n't</u> find <u>no</u> trousers' sounds <u>wrong</u> because it is.

4) '<u>No</u>ne' is like 'no' — it <u>doesn't work</u> with '<u>-n't</u>' or '<u>not</u>'.

 Polly does<u>n't</u> have <u>any</u> to give him. ✓

'Polly does<u>n't</u> have <u>none</u> to give him' <u>wouldn't make sense</u>.

'Does<u>n't</u>', is the <u>only negative</u>, so the sentence is <u>correct</u>.

You should treat the words '<u>no</u>ne', '<u>no</u>thing' and '<u>no</u>where' like the word '<u>no</u>'.

Don't use 'ain't'

1) 'Ain't' is a word you hear <u>spoken or sung</u> quite a lot, but you <u>shouldn't use</u> it in <u>written English</u>. Instead you should use '<u>hasn't</u>', '<u>isn't</u>', '<u>haven't</u>' or '<u>am not</u>'.

2) If you're not sure which one of them to use, <u>try each one</u> until it <u>sounds right</u>.

 That <u>isn't</u> fair.   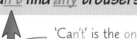 *I <u>haven't</u> seen it.*   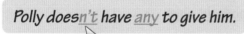 *It <u>hasn't</u> arrived.*   *I'm <u>not</u> hungry.*

Using '<u>ain't</u>' with any of these sentences would be <u>incorrect</u>.

If it ain't broke, don't fix it — ahem, if it isn't broken...

<u>Double negatives</u> are things to watch out for in your <u>sentences</u> — if you're trying to put a <u>negative</u> in a sentence, then make sure you only use <u>one</u> '<u>no</u>' or '<u>not</u>'. Don't even think about using '<u>ain't</u>'.

Negatives

There's a bit more to learn about <u>negatives</u>, but on the <u>positive</u> side, you've <u>nearly finished</u>...

Don't confuse 'don't' and 'doesn't'

'<u>Doesn't</u>' is short for '<u>does not</u>' — you use it with '<u>he</u>', '<u>she</u>' and '<u>it</u>', or when using the <u>name</u> of <u>one person</u> or <u>thing</u>.

She <u>doesn't</u> live here.

Ahmed <u>doesn't</u> care about rugby.

It <u>doesn't</u> rain on the plains.

'<u>Don't</u>' is short for '<u>do not</u>'. Use it if you're writing about <u>more than one person or thing</u>.

They <u>don't</u> understand French.

His dogs <u>don't</u> like cheese.

'<u>Don't</u>' is also used in sentences with '<u>you</u>' or '<u>I</u>'.

You <u>don't</u> need to go there.

I <u>don't</u> agree with your talking parrot.

Use the long form to check you're right

The easiest way to <u>check</u> which one is <u>right</u> is to use the <u>long form</u> ('<u>does not</u>' or '<u>do not</u>') and see what <u>sounds right</u>.

Test the sentence by turning '<u>don't</u>' into '<u>do not</u>' and '<u>does not</u>'.

We <u>don't</u> have any dolphins.

We <u>do not</u> have any dolphins. ✓ This <u>makes sense</u>, so '<u>don't</u>' has been used <u>correctly</u>.

We <u>does not</u> have any dolphins. ✗ This <u>doesn't make sense</u>, so it would be incorrect to use '<u>doesn't</u>'.

Let's test the sentence...

Isaac <u>doesn't</u> work very hard.

Isaac <u>do not</u> work very hard. ✗ This <u>doesn't sound right</u>, so you can't use '<u>don't</u>'.

Isaac <u>does not</u> work very hard. ✓ This <u>makes sense</u>, so '<u>doesn't</u>' has been used <u>correctly</u>.

My compass can sometimes be quite negative...

Remember, if you're writing about <u>one person or thing</u> then use '<u>doesn't</u>'. If it's <u>more than one</u>, use '<u>don't</u>'. '<u>You</u>' and '<u>I</u>' always use '<u>don't</u>'. There's even an easy test to tell you've used the right one.

Revision Summary Questions

There we are — our thrilling ride through the world of basic grammar has come to a close. That can only mean one thing — it's time for some questions...

1) Write down which of these words are proper nouns, which are common nouns and which are abstract nouns:
   a) horse   b) chimney   c) freedom   d) Mr Smith   e) December

2) Put 'a' or 'an' in front of each of these words:
   a) company   b) igloo   c) umbrella   d) unicorn   e) newspaper

3) Replace the underlined words in these sentences with a suitable pronoun:
   a) <u>Jane</u> likes <u>sport</u>.   c) <u>Spiders</u> eat <u>flies</u>.   e) <u>Harry</u> looks at <u>Tina</u>.
   b) Those are <u>Harold's socks</u>.   d) His hand touched <u>Anna's</u>.   f) That's not <u>your pen</u>.

4) Rewrite these sentences using the correct underlined word so that they make sense.
   a) Pam and <u>me</u> / <u>I</u> left.   b) Kareem gave <u>me</u> / <u>I</u> a pen.   c) Tell <u>me</u> / <u>I</u> the truth.

5) Add 'which' or 'who' to these sentences so that they make sense:
   a) Henry had a friend ___ was called Percy.   b) I've got an itch ___ is just out of reach.

6) Rewrite these sentences, using the correct underlined word, so that they make sense.
   a) Bill is the man <u>who</u> / <u>whom</u> buys the milk.   b) To <u>who</u> / <u>whom</u> did you write?

7) Rewrite these sentences, using the correct underlined word, so that they make sense.
   a) <u>Who's</u> / <u>Whose</u> going to the party?   b) <u>Who's</u> / <u>Whose</u> bag is this?

8) Rewrite these sentences with the correct present tense form of the verbs in brackets.
   a) I (to chase) rabbits in the park.   b) She (to like) chocolate.   c) We (to sing) carols.

9) Add commas to these sentences where they are needed:
   a) Sarah has straight light blonde hair.   b) Big grumpy fluffy lions are watching me.

10) Which of these words are adverbs and which are adjectives?
   a) friendly   b) badly   c) crazily   d) silly   e) very

11) Which of these statements are sentences, and which are not?
   a) He made a cake.   b) At six o'clock.   c) Tell me more.   d) Not now.

12) Which of these statements are phrases, and which are clauses?
   a) In the dark   b) By himself   c) Karl tickles Snowy   d) Take me home

13) Which of these statements are main clauses, and which are subordinate clauses?
   a) Sid plays golf   b) Because of the sun   c) Whilst singing   d) They fell down

14) Add the prepositions 'at', 'in', 'since' and 'on' to these sentences so that they make sense:
   Our kitchen is a mess. There are dirty dishes ___ the sink and boxes ___ the floor.
   It's been like this ___ March. There's no space for us to cook ___ teatime.

15) List the conjunctions that the word 'FANBOYS' refers to.

16) Rewrite this confusing passage by adding paragraphs so that it's easier to read:

   The biggest challenge facing Junior League Football today is the sheer number of red and yellow cards issued by referees. There is no doubt that standards of discipline have fallen sharply. Last year, 85 yellow cards and 14 red cards were issued in the first six weeks of the season. In comparison, 136 yellow cards and 26 red cards have already been issued this year. Many players are facing a four-match ban. Hector Dalrymple, Chairman of the UK Federation of Under-16 Football Clubs, claimed the situation was reaching crisis point.

17) Correct these sentences:
   a) There ain't no food in the fridge.   b) I doesn't know.   c) She don't work here.

Writing About Time

This page is all about <u>time</u>, but it's about <u>verbs</u> too, so have a read of <u>p.44-45</u> if you need to.

Changing *the* verb changes *the* time

1) If you want to write about something that <u>is happening</u>, <u>has happened</u>, or <u>will happen</u> in the future, you need to <u>make sure</u> your <u>verbs</u> are in the <u>correct tense</u>.

2) A verb's <u>tense</u> tells you <u>when</u> something happens. These are the <u>three main tenses</u> you need to know:

1 Present Tense

I <u>work</u> in a pie shop.

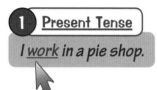

This is the <u>present tense</u> — it's talking about something that is happening <u>now</u>.

2 Past Tense

I <u>worked</u> in a pie shop.

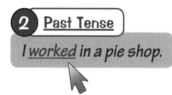

This is the <u>past tense</u> — it's talking about something that has happened.

3 Future Tense

I <u>will work</u> in a pie shop.

This is the <u>future tense</u> — it's talking about something that will happen <u>in the future</u>.

Different tenses *put things in* different times

The different <u>tenses</u> can be used <u>differently</u> to mean <u>different things</u>:

PRESENT

The <u>present tense</u> can show something that is <u>done regularly</u>.

Bill <u>reads</u> comic books. This is something that Bill does <u>regularly</u>, even if he is not doing it <u>right now</u>.

The <u>present tense</u> can also show that something is <u>happening at the moment</u>.

This describes what Bill is doing <u>right now</u>. *Bill is <u>reading</u> a comic book.*

PAST

The <u>past tense</u> describes things that <u>have happened</u>, or <u>used to happen</u> regularly.

Ruby <u>washed</u> the car. This is something that <u>happened</u> in the <u>past</u>.

I <u>played</u> the violin. This is something that <u>used to happen</u> regularly, but <u>doesn't</u> happen anymore.

The <u>past tense</u> can also describe something that <u>has just happened</u>.

This is something that <u>has just happened</u>. *Ruby <u>has washed</u> the car.*

FUTURE

The <u>future tense</u> talks about things that <u>will happen</u> in the <u>future</u>.

Mark <u>will see</u> Saleem tomorrow. This is something that <u>is going to happen</u> in the <u>future</u>.

It's about time you learnt this page...

There we are — Section 5 is up and running and we've got lots to learn about how to <u>change verbs</u> into their <u>different tenses</u>. Make sure you're happy about what a <u>tense</u> is and then <u>crack on</u>.

Writing About Now

Now you know what a <u>tense</u> is, it's time to <u>get cracking</u> on the <u>present tense</u>...

Most verbs follow a pattern

1) The <u>present tense</u> is easy to form — <u>most verbs don't change</u> at all.

2) You only <u>change</u> the verb when the subject is '<u>he</u>', '<u>she</u>' or '<u>it</u>'.
With 'he', 'she' and 'it', you have to <u>add</u> an '<u>-s</u>' to the <u>end of the verb</u>.

<u>to love</u>

<u>I love</u> **Bruno.** <u>You love</u> **Bruno.** <u>We love</u> **Bruno.** <u>They love</u> **Bruno.**

<u>He loves</u> **Bruno.** <u>She loves</u> **Bruno.** <u>It loves</u> **Bruno.**

You need to add '<u>-s</u>' for '<u>he</u>', '<u>she</u>' and '<u>it</u>'.

I hope ➡ He hope<u>s</u>   You hide ➡ She hide<u>s</u>   We make ➡ It make<u>s</u>

You have to be more careful with some verbs

1) Some <u>irregular</u> verbs <u>don't follow</u> this present tense <u>pattern</u>.

2) Two of the most <u>common ones</u> are '<u>to be</u>' and '<u>to have</u>'. You just <u>need to learn</u> them:

These are <u>auxiliary</u> (or <u>helping</u>) <u>verbs</u>. They can be used to <u>alter</u> the <u>tenses</u> of <u>other verbs</u>.

to <u>be</u>

I am   We are   They are

two bees

You are   He/She/It is

to <u>have</u>

I have   We have   You have

They have   He/She/It has

3) There are some other <u>slightly irregular verbs</u> that need more doing to them when the subject is <u>he</u>, <u>she</u> or <u>it</u>.

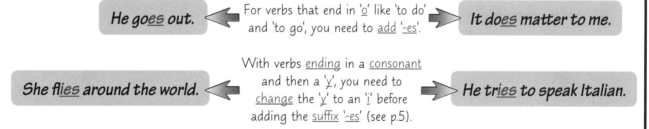

He go<u>es</u> out.   For verbs that end in '<u>o</u>' like 'to do' and 'to go', you need to <u>add</u> '<u>-es</u>'.   It do<u>es</u> matter to me.

She fl<u>ies</u> around the world.   With verbs <u>ending</u> in a <u>consonant</u> and then a '<u>y</u>', you need to <u>change</u> the '<u>y</u>' to an '<u>i</u>' before adding the <u>suffix</u> '<u>-es</u>' (see p.5).   He tr<u>ies</u> to speak Italian.

The present tense — being nervous at Christmas...

Chances are you're already quite <u>familiar</u> with the <u>present tense</u>, but it's easy to make <u>silly mistakes</u> if you don't concentrate, so make sure you <u>really know</u> this page before moving on.

Using '-ing' Verbs

Right about now you must be wondering what this page is all about — let's have a look...

The '-ing' verb says what *is happening*

1) When you want to talk about an action that is still happening, you need to use the present form of the verb 'to be' (see p.59) plus the main verb in its '-ing' form.

2) This basically means you need 'am', 'are' or 'is', and the main verb with '-ing' on the end.

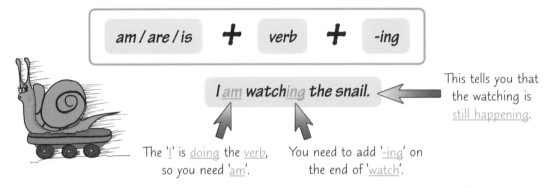

am / are / is **+** verb **+** -ing

I *am* watching the snail.

This tells you that the watching is still happening.

The 'I' is doing the verb, so you need 'am'.

You need to add '-ing' on the end of 'watch'.

Most verbs just *need '-ing'*

A long vowel sound is when a vowel has a strong sound, like in 'keep' or 'house'. They often have the same sound as the letter of the alphabet, e.g. 'e' sounds like 'ee'.

To make most verbs talk about what is still happening, you just need to add '-ing' on the end.

1) Verbs which have a long vowel sound:

sleep → *They are sleeping.*

'Ee' is a long vowel sound.

So you just add '-ing' to the end of the verb.

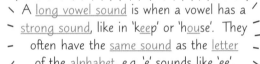
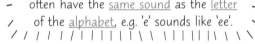

rain → *It is raining.*

The 'ai' is a long vowel sound.

So you just add '-ing' to the end.

2) Verbs ending with two consonants:

talk → *He is talking.*

'Talk' ends in '-lk' — two consonants.

So '-ing' is just added to the end.

melt → *It's melting.*

'Melt' ends in two consonants.

So it becomes 'melting' — easy.

3) Verbs which end with two vowels (except for 'ie'):

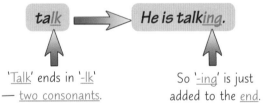

free → *We are freeing them.*

'Free' ends in two vowels.

The '-ing' is added straight onto the 'ee'.

see → *She is seeing.*

'See' ends in 'ee' — two vowels.

Just stick '-ing' on the end, like the rest.

'-ing' is king if you want to know what's happening...

I'm afraid to say that this is the easy page about adding '-ing' to verbs — the next one is a bit trickier. But for now, enjoy adding '-ing' without a care in the world, or a verb to be changed.

Using '-ing' Verbs

We've got some <u>doubling</u> and some <u>dropping</u> coming up — don't get them <u>mixed up</u>.

Some words *double* the *final consonant*

1) When you've got a <u>verb</u> with a <u>short vowel sound</u> like '<u>dig</u>' or '<u>slip</u>', you need to <u>double the final consonant</u> before adding the '<u>-ing</u>'.

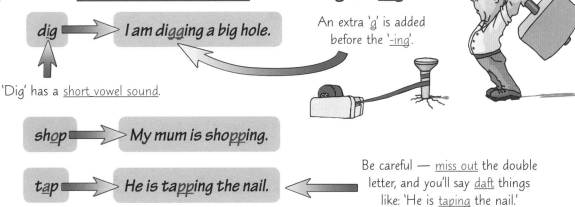

dig ➡ *I am digging a big hole.*

An extra '<u>g</u>' is added before the '<u>-ing</u>'.

'Dig' has a <u>short vowel sound</u>.

shop ➡ *My mum is shopping.*

tap ➡ *He is tapping the nail.*

Be careful — <u>miss out</u> the double letter, and you'll say <u>daft</u> things like: 'He is <u>taping</u> the nail.'

2) There are some longer words (e.g. '<u>offer</u>' — '<u>offering</u>') that <u>don't double</u> the <u>final consonant</u>. Have a flick to <u>p.5-6</u> for some extra info on <u>adding suffixes</u> to words.

Some verbs *drop* the *final 'e' before adding '-ing'*

1) Verbs that end in a <u>silent 'e'</u> drop it before adding '<u>-ing</u>'.

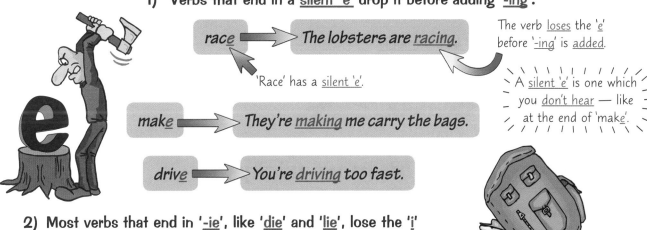

race ➡ *The lobsters are <u>racing</u>.*

The verb <u>loses</u> the '<u>e</u>' before '<u>-ing</u>' is added.

'Race' has a <u>silent 'e'</u>.

A <u>silent 'e'</u> is one which you <u>don't hear</u> — like at the end of '<u>make</u>'.

make ➡ *They're <u>making</u> me carry the bags.*

drive ➡ *You're <u>driving</u> too fast.*

2) Most verbs that end in '<u>-ie</u>', like '<u>die</u>' and '<u>lie</u>', lose the '<u>i</u>' and '<u>e</u>' and <u>replace</u> them with a '<u>y</u>' before adding '<u>-ing</u>'.

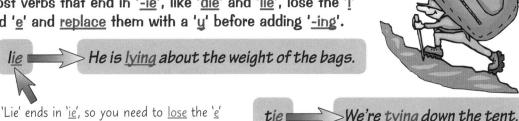

lie ➡ *He is <u>lying</u> about the weight of the bags.*

'Lie' ends in '<u>ie</u>', so you need to <u>lose</u> the '<u>e</u>' and <u>replace</u> the '<u>i</u>' with a '<u>y</u>'. Then you can <u>add</u> '<u>-ing</u>' to the <u>end</u> of the verb.

tie ➡ *We're <u>tying</u> down the tent.*

Finally a page about getting rid of final 'e's...

This is a <u>crucial</u> page to remember and it will make a <u>big difference</u> to your writing if you can remember <u>when</u> to <u>double the final consonant</u> and when to get rid of the <u>final 'e' or 'ie'</u>.

Writing About the Past

Ahh, the <u>past</u> — those were the days... Learn this page so you can <u>write about them</u> like me.

Most verbs just need '-ed' to become the simple past

1) To make <u>most verbs</u> into the <u>simple past</u> you just add '<u>-ed</u>' on the end.

> walk ➡ *He walk<u>ed</u> ten miles.*

The verb has had '<u>-ed</u>' added to it — it's now in the <u>past tense</u>. The walking has <u>already happened</u>.

2) If a verb <u>doubles its final consonant</u> when '<u>-ing</u>' is added, you also need to <u>double it</u> when '<u>-ed</u>' is added.

> *He so<u>bbed</u> like a baby.*

An extra '<u>b</u>' is added to '<u>sob</u>' when '<u>-ed</u>' is added to make it <u>past tense</u>.

What's his problem?

Some verbs need a 't' instead of an '-ed'

Some past tense verbs can end in <u>either</u> '<u>-ed</u>' or '<u>-t</u>' — e.g. 'learnt' and 'learned'.

1) Some verbs need a '<u>-t</u>' on the end instead of '<u>-ed</u>' to make them <u>past tense</u>. The best thing to do is to <u>learn them</u>:

> deal ➡ deal<u>t</u>   mean ➡ mean<u>t</u>   burn ➡ burn<u>t</u>   learn ➡ learn<u>t</u>

2) Some verbs that <u>end</u> in '<u>ll</u>' need to <u>drop</u> an '<u>l</u>' before <u>adding</u> '<u>-t</u>':

> spe<u>l</u>l ➡ spe<u>l</u>t   spi<u>l</u>l ➡ spi<u>l</u>t   sme<u>l</u>l ➡ sme<u>l</u>t

3) Most verbs with '<u>ee</u>' in the <u>middle</u> <u>lose</u> an '<u>e</u>' and <u>get</u> a '<u>-t</u>' on the <u>end</u>:

> sl<u>ee</u>p ➡ sl<u>e</u>p<u>t</u>   keep ➡ k<u>e</u>p<u>t</u>

Some verbs are a bit more tricky

Unfortunately there are lots of <u>irregular verbs</u> that you just need to <u>learn</u>.

Watch out for verbs that <u>don't change</u> at all — e.g. 'cut', 'hit', 'put', 'beat', 'set' and 'let'.

see ➡ <u>saw</u>	make ➡ <u>made</u>	do ➡ <u>did</u>	
steal ➡ <u>stole</u>	eat ➡ <u>ate</u>	have ➡ <u>had</u>	
wear ➡ <u>wore</u>	take ➡ <u>took</u>	think ➡ <u>thought</u>	get ➡ <u>got</u>
come ➡ <u>came</u>	fight ➡ <u>fought</u>	be ➡ <u>was / were</u>	go ➡ <u>went</u>

I only eat verbs — I'm a verbivore...

Those <u>verbs</u> won't like it if you don't put them into the <u>past tense</u> properly, so get <u>learning</u>.

The Past Tense with 'Have'

You need to be <u>sure</u> about the verb '<u>to have</u>' for this page. If you're not, then <u>p.59</u> will help.

Past tense *with 'have' is different to the simple past*

1) You use the <u>past tense with 'have'</u> to talk about something that has <u>happened recently</u>.

> They <u>have burnt</u> the potatoes.

> He <u>has finished</u> the race.

This means that the race has <u>recently finished</u>. You wouldn't use it to talk about a race from last year.

2) To <u>form</u> the past tense with 'have', you need the present form of the verb 'to have' (so '<u>have</u>' or '<u>has</u>') and then the <u>past tense with 'have'</u> form of the main <u>verb</u>.

> has / have **+** past tense with 'have' verb form

> The shark <u>has arrived</u>.

This tells you that the arriving has <u>finished</u> happening <u>recently</u>.

'<u>Has</u>' is used because there's one <u>shark</u>.

'<u>Arrived</u>' is the <u>past tense with 'have'</u> verb form.

You must learn these tricky common ones

1) Most verbs are <u>spelt the same</u> in the simple past and the <u>past tense with 'have' form</u>, even though the <u>meaning</u> is <u>different</u>.

> Michael <u>spilt</u> his drink. ➡ Michael <u>has spilt</u> his drink.

'Spilt' is <u>spelt the same</u>, but the <u>meaning has changed</u>.

2) Some verbs <u>change</u> in the <u>past tense with 'have' form</u>.

> They <u>ate</u> the cookies. ➡ They <u>have eaten</u> the cookies.

In its <u>past tense with 'have' form</u>, '<u>ate</u>' changes to '<u>eaten</u>'.

Learn these common forms:

> <u>take</u> ➡ It <u>has taken</u> too long.
> <u>go</u> ➡ She <u>has gone</u> to Belgium.
> <u>write</u> ➡ I <u>have written</u> a book.
> <u>do</u> ➡ We <u>have done</u> all we can.

> <u>give</u> ➡ I <u>have given</u> Roger an apple.
> <u>show</u> ➡ He <u>has shown</u> me the core.
> <u>be</u> ➡ It <u>has been</u> a pleasure.
> <u>have</u> ➡ I <u>have had</u> a great time.

I have finished, you have finished, we have finished...

... this page. Some more verbs that need <u>learning</u>, but on the <u>plus side</u> you should now be an <u>expert</u> at sports commentating and news reading — they both use the <u>past tense with 'have'</u> a lot.

The Past Tense with 'Have'

'Been', 'seen' and 'done' are used incorrectly all the time, so this is a good page to read.

With 'been' or 'seen' you need to use 'has' or 'have'

If you use 'been' or 'seen' then you always need to use 'have' or 'has' with them, otherwise the sentence won't make sense.

> I have been working.

> We have seen an elephant recently.

> She has seen that film eleven times.

> It has been eating lots.

'She seen that film' doesn't make sense — you need to use 'has'.

When you write 'done' you also need 'has' or 'have'

1) The word 'done' also needs 'has' or 'have' with it every time you use it.

> They have done a great job. ⟸ 'They done a great job' doesn't make sense as a sentence — you need the 'have'.

2) You can also use 'did' instead of 'have done' — you don't need 'has' or 'have' with 'did'.

> I have done my training.   OR   I did my training. ⟸ 'I have did' wouldn't make sense — 'did' doesn't need 'has' or 'have'.

Don't confuse 'been' / 'being' or 'seen' / 'seeing'

1) Even though they sound similar, 'been' and 'being' are different tenses.

2) 'Been' needs 'has' or 'have' with it, whereas 'being' needs 'is' / 'was' or 'are' / 'were'.

> He has been to America. ⟸ With 'been' you always need 'have' or 'has'.

'She has being' or 'she being' wouldn't make sense. You need to use 'is' or 'was'. ⟹ She is being annoying.

3) It's the same with 'seen' and 'seeing' — 'seen' needs 'has' or 'have', 'seeing' needs 'is' / 'was' or 'are' / 'were'.

> I have seen the Grand Canyon. ⟸ With 'seen' you always need 'have' or 'has'.

'We have seeing' or 'We seeing' wouldn't make sense — you need to use 'are' or 'were'. ⟹ We are seeing some friends.

Been there, done that, seen the T-shirt...

It's pretty important that you remember which words need that little 'have' or 'has' before them — leave them out and your sentences won't make sense, and that would be sad for everyone...

Have and Of

Of course we had to have a page about these two little words — handle them with care.

It's easy to confuse 'have' and 'of'

1) Have a look at these sentences:

> We could have won the cup.   She might have lost her shoes.

2) It seems like 'could of' and 'might of' could be used here because they sound similar to 'could've' and 'might've'.

3) However, 'could of' and 'might of' are wrong — you shouldn't use them in your writing.

You can't put 'could of' into this sentence — it has to be 'could have'. ➡️ He could have played in an orchestra.

Use 'have' not 'of'

1) It's easy to get 'have' and 'of' muddled up, so it will help to learn the verbs that use 'have'.

2) The verbs in the sentences below often use 'have' but never use 'of'.

may ➡️ We may have been upset.

> These are all examples of modal verbs. Modal verbs suggest how likely it is that something will happen.

must ➡️ It must have broken.

shall ➡️ I shall have read it by tonight.

would ➡️ He would have won.

should ➡️ Ceri should have been there.

could ➡️ Sophia could have gone.

might ➡️ I might have been awake.

3) A good trick is to remember that 'have' is a verb, so it usually follows other doing words:

He could have played at Buckingham Palace. ⬅️ 'Have' follows another verb — 'could'.

4) 'Of' is a preposition (see p.51), not a verb. You'd use it in phrases like:

lots of fish   pack of cards   because of this

Should have, would have, could have — such regrets...

The basic message of this page is summed up nicely in that yellow box about halfway down: 'Use 'have' not 'of''. 'Of' simply doesn't belong with words like 'could', 'might' and 'should'.

Staying in the Right Tense

You'd be surprised at how easy it is to <u>mix up</u> your <u>tenses</u> in a sentence. But this will <u>help</u>...

Stay in the same tense in your writing

Once you've picked a <u>tense</u>, you usually need to stick with it. All the <u>verbs</u> need to <u>agree</u> with <u>each other</u>.

> I <u>live</u> in a town where there <u>are</u> lots of purple squirrels.

'<u>Live</u>' and '<u>are</u>' are both in the <u>present tense</u> — they <u>agree</u> with each other.

> When we <u>went</u> to Ireland we <u>saw</u> green squirrels and we <u>eat</u> some purple kiwis.

'<u>Went</u>' and '<u>saw</u>' are both in the <u>past tense</u> — they <u>agree</u> with each other.

'<u>Eat</u>' is in the <u>present tense</u>, so the sentence <u>doesn't make sense</u> — the verb should be '<u>ate</u>'.

The past tense describes what's already happened

If you're <u>writing</u> about something that happened in the <u>past</u>, then <u>all</u> of your <u>verbs</u> need to be in the <u>past tense</u>.

> British pandas <u>moved</u> to China in 1791. They <u>left</u> Britain because they <u>were made</u> to wear top hats on Sundays. They <u>argued</u> that this <u>was</u> unfair, but the government <u>kept</u> the law in place.

All these verbs are in the <u>past tense</u>. It <u>makes sense</u> and it's clear that these things have <u>already happened</u>.

Be careful with the present

When you're writing in the <u>present tense</u>, be <u>careful</u> not to <u>mix up</u> past and present verbs. Keep <u>everything</u> in the <u>same tense</u>.

Because this is in the <u>present tense</u>, all of the verbs are in the present tense too.

> There <u>is</u> a friendly mole that <u>lives</u> at the bottom of my garden. His name <u>is</u> Marcus and he <u>plays</u> hide-and-seek with my chickens. He <u>digs</u> about five holes every night.

It's clear that all these things are <u>still happening</u>. There are <u>no past tense verbs</u> hiding in there.

Staying in the right tents — crucial camping advice...

Now that you've spent all this time learning how to use <u>tenses</u>, it would be a <u>shame</u> if you <u>mixed</u> them all up in your <u>writing</u>. The <u>rules</u> are quite <u>easy</u> though — if you want to write in the <u>present</u>, make sure <u>all of your verbs</u> are in the <u>present tense</u>. It's the same for the <u>past</u>. Cracking.

Revision Summary Questions

Time to put all that you've learnt into practice. It might not be the most fun thing to do with your time, but I guarantee that it's the best way to check that you've taken everything in. Give the questions a crack on your own first, but if you get really stuck then you can always revisit the pages in this section.

1) For each of the sentences below, write down what tense they are in:
   a) There was an earthquake.   b) I will visit Granny tomorrow.   c) Andy plays volleyball.

2) Rewrite these sentences with the correct present tense form of the verbs in brackets.
   E.g. Mark (to tell) Greg the story. ⟶ Mark <u>tells</u> Greg the story.
   a) Kareema (to go) to badminton club.
   b) Mrs Tunstall (to bake) delicious cakes.
   c) I (to have) a sore throat.
   d) A butterfly (to fly) around our garden.
   e) Happiness (to be) the key to success.
   f) Frogs (to swim) in our pond.

3) Rewrite the sentences below, changing the underlined verbs into their '-ing' form.
   E.g. His bag <u>lies</u> on the floor. ⟶ His bag <u>is lying</u> on the floor.
   a) Mrs Busy-Body <u>peeps</u> over the fence.
   b) Miss Obedient <u>agrees</u> with you.
   c) Lady Tango <u>dances</u> to music.
   d) Mr Outdoorsy <u>walks</u> to the park.
   e) Master Scout <u>plans</u> his route.
   f) Sir Fibber <u>lies</u> to his wife.

4) Rewrite these sentences with the correct past tense form of the verbs in brackets.
   E.g. It (to begin) to rain. ⟶ It <u>began</u> to rain.
   a) I (to stop) the car.
   b) Sheila (to clean) her desk.
   c) Oscar (to see) his teacher dancing.
   d) They (to change) their clothes.
   e) My brother (to lend) me his bike.
   f) Kam (to go) to London last week.
   g) The pop stars (to meet) their fans.
   h) We (to cut) our hair last night.

5) Rewrite the sentences below, changing the underlined verbs into their 'past tense with have' form.
   E.g. Naomi <u>shouts</u> at the girls. ⟶ Naomi <u>has shouted</u> at the girls.
   a) Miriam <u>hits</u> Alf.
   b) We <u>go</u> to bed.
   c) The birds <u>eat</u> the seeds.
   d) The boys <u>climb</u> the tree.
   e) Mustafa <u>plays</u> cards.
   f) Tyrone <u>writes</u> a letter.

6) Rewrite the sentences below so that they make sense:
   E.g. Amit not done his homework. ⟶ Amit <u>has</u> not <u>done</u> his homework.
   a) They seen the film.
   b) I done all my work.
   c) Franklin and Geoff been swimming.
   d) Mr Potts has did the housework.
   e) Jared seen the new plans.
   f) You done the washing?

7) Circle the correct underlined word in each of these sentences so that they make sense:
   a) Faye was <u>being</u> / <u>been</u> very silly.
   b) Dev was just <u>being</u> / <u>been</u> awkward.
   c) The children were <u>seen</u> / <u>seeing</u> Granny.
   d) The judges have <u>seeing</u> / <u>seen</u> the band.

8) Circle the correct underlined word in each of these sentences so that they make sense:
   a) Simon thought <u>have</u> / <u>of</u> a great idea.
   b) The fans should <u>have</u> / <u>of</u> shouted more.
   c) The party may <u>have</u> / <u>of</u> been cancelled.
   d) The opposition could <u>have</u> / <u>of</u> tried harder.
   e) He's never heard <u>have</u> / <u>of</u> that.
   f) The winners might <u>have</u> / <u>of</u> celebrated.

9) The tenses in the passage below aren't consistent. Rewrite it with the correct tense.
   Last year we went to Madrid and we visit my friends. We swam in their pool, play tennis and eat paella. We see the opera house and the cathedral. My sister and I took a trip on the city tour bus. When we got off, we look around the 'Museo del Prado' (a big art gallery). I spoke a bit of Spanish and try lots of different food. I also met lots of people and make lots of new friends. It was a great trip!

Writing in Standard English

Ever wondered about the <u>differences</u> between <u>Standard</u> and <u>non-Standard English</u>? I have...

Standard **and** *non-Standard English* **are different**

1) <u>Standard English</u> follows <u>spelling</u>, <u>punctuation</u> and <u>grammar</u> rules.
    It's a more <u>formal</u> type of English.

2) <u>Non-Standard English</u> doesn't follow formal <u>spelling</u>, <u>punctuation</u> and <u>grammar</u> rules.
    It's a more <u>informal</u> type of English.

Non-Standard English **is found in** *speech*

1) People sometimes use <u>non-Standard English</u> when they speak.
    You need to use <u>Standard English</u> in your writing.

I <u>ain't</u> sure. ✗ ➡ I <u>am not</u> sure. ✓   They <u>is</u> dragons. ✗ ➡ They <u>are</u> dragons. ✓

I'm <u>well</u> happy. ✗ ➡ I'm <u>really</u> happy. ✓   We haven't got <u>none</u>. ✗ ➡ We haven't got <u>any</u>. ✓

2) Using <u>Standard English</u> makes your writing <u>clear</u> and <u>easy</u> to understand. It's good
    for most types of writing, and especially for <u>serious</u> things like a letter of complaint.

3) Using <u>non-Standard English</u> can make your writing more <u>friendly</u>, so you might use it
    to write to a friend. However, using <u>non-Standard English</u> might also make people think
    you <u>can't use SPaG correctly</u>, so it's best to <u>stick</u> to <u>Standard English</u> for most work.

Stick to Standard English **most of the time**

The <u>only</u> time you should use <u>non-Standard English</u> in your work is for <u>creative</u>
<u>writing</u>. Non-Standard English can help <u>shape</u> a character — it can tell the
reader more about the character's <u>background</u> and what <u>they're like</u>:

> The sky had turned dark, the clouds had drawn in and the waves thrashed violently
> against the shore. With a crash, Captain Buck's ship ploughed into the beach.
>
> "Get yer miserable selves off me ship and find me that treasure! You ain't comin' back
> on board 'til yer do!" boomed Captain Buck.
>
> The pirates launched themselves onto the beach and began walking towards the
> rocks. Without a word, they headed into the deepest cave. Suddenly, the silence was
> broken by the loud squawks of McDonnel's parrot.
>
> "Find me treasure! Find me treasure!"
>
> "Shut up, you feather-brained fool!" hissed McDonnel in a loud whisper.

This text has a <u>mixture</u> of <u>Standard</u> and <u>non-Standard English</u>.

Standard English is used for <u>setting the scene</u>.

Non-Standard English is used for the <u>characters' speech</u> — it makes the <u>characters</u> seem more <u>real</u> and makes the story more <u>interesting</u>.

You could write <u>all</u> of a story in non-Standard English if the whole
thing is written from the <u>perspective</u> of one of your <u>characters</u>.

Using Standard English — it's standard practice...

There's often a big <u>difference</u> between the English we <u>speak</u> and the English we <u>write</u>.
What you <u>say</u> isn't always <u>suitable</u> for <u>written</u> work. Remember this and you won't slip up...

Writing in the Right Style

The <u>style</u> you choose to write in is pretty <u>important</u>. Read on and you'll find out why...

You can write in a formal or informal style

1) A <u>formal style</u> seems <u>serious</u>. It usually <u>doesn't</u> sound like it's talking <u>directly</u> to someone.

2) An <u>informal style</u> sounds more <u>friendly</u> and <u>chatty</u>.
It often sounds like it's talking <u>directly</u> to the reader.

> I hate being formal.

Homework must be handed in immediately. ← A <u>formal style</u>.

An <u>informal style</u>. → *Chop-chop — it's time to hand in your homework.*

I <u>received</u> your letter. <u>Thank you</u>. → *<u>Got</u> your letter. <u>Ta</u>.*

They <u>are stealing</u> a DVD. → *<u>They're nicking</u> a DVD.*

<u>Informal</u> writing often uses <u>slang</u> and <u>shortened words</u>, but <u>formal</u> writing <u>doesn't</u>.

A formal style is used for serious writing

1) If you're writing something to someone <u>important</u>, or to someone you <u>don't know</u> very well, use a <u>formal style</u>. This might include a <u>letter</u>, an <u>essay</u> or a <u>report</u>.

2) You should <u>normally</u> use a <u>formal</u> style in your <u>writing</u>, unless you need to write <u>informally</u> for a piece of <u>creative writing</u>.

An Informal style is used for more friendly writing

If you're writing something to someone you <u>know</u> well, you might use an <u>informal style</u>.
Here's an example of when an informal style could be used:

The style of the article is <u>friendly</u>.

Grove Hill High Gazette
Pupil Power!

<u>Many of us here at Grove Hill</u> will already know about the battle to save 'Old Oaky'. The council's plan to cut down <u>our famous tree</u> has been the <u>talk of the school</u> for weeks.
Today, the Gazette can reveal that the council has decided not to chop down the tree after all.

Kieran Ford, who led the 'Save Oaky' campaign, told the Gazette that he <u>couldn't</u> have done it without the support of <u>all you Grovers</u>.
The Council obviously <u>met its match</u> when it came up against <u>our school</u>. All <u>that's</u> left to say is: <u>Go Grove Hill High!</u>

The article uses <u>shortened words</u>.

The author sounds like they're speaking <u>directly</u> to the reader.

It uses <u>spoken expressions</u>.

This article is written in <u>Standard English</u>, as it needs to be <u>clear</u>, but it has an <u>informal style</u>. The author <u>knows</u> their <u>audience</u> well, so an informal style is okay.

I'm trying to be friendly, so I've gone totally informal...
The <u>style</u> of the English we use affects <u>how</u> it is read. Getting the style <u>wrong</u> can cause <u>problems</u>.

Choosing Active or Passive

Writing in <u>active</u> or <u>passive</u> sentences can <u>change</u> the <u>effect</u> of your <u>writing</u>.

*Active sentences **focus on who***

1) In active sentences it's clear <u>who</u> is doing the action (<u>the subject</u>) because they usually come just <u>before</u> the <u>verb</u>. Remember that the <u>verb</u> must <u>agree</u> with the <u>subject</u> of the sentence — in active sentences that's the <u>person</u> doing the <u>action</u>.

<u>'My puppy'</u> is <u>doing</u> the action — he's the <u>subject</u>.

<u>My puppy</u> chases <u>the boy</u>.

'The boy' is having the action done <u>to him</u> — he's the <u>object</u>.

'<u>Puppy</u>' is <u>singular</u>, so the verb (to chase) is also <u>singular</u>.

2) You should usually use <u>active sentences</u> in your writing — they're much <u>clearer</u> and make your writing <u>easier</u> to <u>read</u>.

*Passive sentences **focus on what***

1) In <u>passive</u> sentences, something is <u>done to</u> the subject.

'<u>The boy</u>' is the <u>subject</u>, even though the action was being done to him.

<u>The boy</u> was chased <u>by</u> the puppy.

The word '<u>by</u>' can introduce <u>who</u> does the action.

2) The <u>verb</u> still needs to <u>agree</u> with the <u>subject</u> — in <u>passive sentences</u> that's the <u>person</u> or <u>thing</u> having the <u>action done to them</u>.

Jim <u>was</u> trapped by Magnus and Scott.

The <u>action</u> was being done to '<u>Jim</u>'. '<u>Jim</u>' is <u>singular</u>, so the <u>verb</u> (to be) is also <u>singular</u>.

3) <u>Passive</u> sentences are useful when you want to:

<u>Emphasise</u> the <u>action</u> — when it's more important to say <u>what</u> the action was, rather than who did it.

The thief was <u>arrested</u> by the police.

Create <u>suspense</u> — in passive sentences you <u>don't</u> always need to say <u>who</u> does the action.

<u>The boy</u> was chased down the street.

I <u>don't</u> want people <u>to know</u> what was chasing the boy until later, so I can <u>leave this bit out</u>. Handy.

Sound <u>bossy</u> — passive sentences can make your tone sound more <u>serious</u>.

All breakages must be reported to reception.   *Parking is prohibited.*

I don't do any exercise, but my sentences are active...

<u>Active</u> sentences are handy little things when you want to <u>focus</u> on <u>who</u> is doing the action. <u>Passive</u> sentences are useful for emphasising <u>what</u> happened. Now that's sorted, let's turn over...

Spelling Tips

It will help you learn tricky spellings if you come up with your <u>own ways</u> of <u>remembering</u> them.

Use mnemonics to jog your memory

1) <u>Mnemonics</u> are <u>sentences</u> or <u>phrases</u> that can <u>help</u> you <u>remember</u> spellings.

2) <u>Making up</u> your own will <u>help</u> you <u>learn</u> words that you find tricky.

3) The <u>first letters</u> of these phrases help you remember how to spell difficult words:

> Rhythm ⇨ <u>R</u>hythm <u>H</u>as <u>Y</u>our <u>T</u>wo <u>H</u>ips <u>M</u>oving

> Necessary ⇨ <u>N</u>ever <u>E</u>at <u>C</u>hips — <u>E</u>at <u>S</u>alad <u>S</u>andwiches <u>A</u>nd <u>R</u>emain <u>Y</u>oung

> Because ⇨ <u>B</u>ig <u>E</u>lephants <u>C</u>an <u>A</u>lways <u>U</u>nderstand <u>S</u>mall <u>E</u>lephants

> Tight, light, sight, fight ⇨ First letter (i.e. 't', 'l', 's' and 'f'), then <u>I</u>'ve <u>G</u>ot <u>H</u>airy <u>T</u>ights

> Could, would, should ⇨ First letter (i.e. 'c', 'w', and 'sh'), then <u>O</u>h <u>U</u> <u>L</u>ittle <u>D</u>arling

Try using funny sentences

> *Remember these smaller words and you'll find it much easier to spell the longer words.*

1) <u>Funny sentences</u> can <u>remind</u> you of <u>spellings</u> you keep <u>forgetting</u>.

> There's <u>a rat</u> in sep<u>arat</u>e.   There's a <u>lie</u> in bel<u>ie</u>f.   The <u>secret</u>ary has a <u>secret</u>.

> You <u>gain</u> when you get a bar<u>gain</u>.   <u>Emma</u> faced a dil<u>emma</u>.

2) You can make <u>special rules</u> for difficult spellings, like words with <u>double letters</u>.

> Ne<u>cess</u>ary ⇨ A shirt has <u>1</u> collar and <u>2</u> sleeves.

> Emba<u>rrass</u> ⇨ <u>2</u> rosy cheeks and <u>2</u> scarlet cheeks.

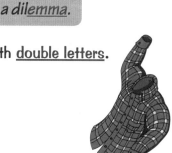

3) Rules for words which <u>sound</u> the <u>same</u> (homophones) are really <u>useful</u>:

> Station<u>er</u>y is for things like pencils and pap<u>er</u>.
> Station<u>ar</u>y is for things that aren't moving, like a p<u>ar</u>ked c<u>ar</u>.

> De<u>ss</u>erts have <u>2</u> <u>s</u>ugar<u>s</u>.
> De<u>s</u>erts just have <u>s</u>and.

Witches are wicked at spelling — they know all the spells...

<u>Remembering</u> how to <u>spell words</u> can be <u>tricky</u>, but <u>mnemonics</u> and <u>funny sentences</u> can make things much <u>easier</u> and much more <u>fun</u>. See how many you can come up with.

Checking Your Work

Now that you've got to grips with SPaG, here are some <u>final tips</u> for <u>checking</u> your work.

Watch out for common spelling mistakes

When you're writing, it's <u>easy</u> to let some common <u>spelling mistakes creep in</u>.

1) Look out for <u>homophones</u> — <u>words</u> which <u>sound the same</u> but are <u>spelt differently</u>:

> *The <u>weather</u> has been awful today.*   *I wonder <u>whether</u> Martin will drive.*

2) Check that you haven't used any <u>text speak</u>.

> *Chocolate is popular <u>because</u> it's delicious.*

Don't write '<u>cos</u>'.

3) Check that you've used <u>letter combinations</u> correctly. Remember the '<u>i before e</u>' rule, check for <u>unstressed vowels</u> and make sure that you've <u>doubled letters</u> where you need to.

Check for obvious punctuation mistakes

1) Make sure that every sentence <u>starts</u> with a <u>capital letter</u> and <u>ends</u> with a <u>full stop</u>.

2) Don't use <u>exclamation marks</u> unless you're sure you need one — you probably <u>won't</u>.

3) Make sure you've added <u>capital letters</u> to words that <u>always</u> need them, like proper nouns:

> *people   towns   countries   characters   titles of books, etc.*

Make sure your grammar *is correct*

1) Check your writing is in the <u>right style</u> for the reader (see p.69).

2) Make sure you don't <u>repeat words</u> like '<u>and</u>', '<u>but</u>' and '<u>because</u>'. Try to use lots of <u>different</u> words. It will help make your writing more interesting.

3) Stick to the <u>same tense</u>. Don't <u>switch</u> between tenses in your writing.

4) Check that you've started a <u>new paragraph</u> every time you talk about a <u>different point</u>, <u>place</u>, <u>person</u> or <u>time</u>. If you <u>forget</u> to start a new paragraph, use a <u>double strike</u> — //.

5) If you know that you often get <u>confused</u> between <u>two words</u>, like 'it's' and 'its', <u>check them</u> extra carefully.

Pen — check. Pencil — check. SPaG — check...

Even Mr Perfect from Perfecton, Perfectshire, Perfectland sometimes makes mistakes — that's why it's a <u>good idea</u> for us all to <u>reread our work</u> and <u>double-check</u> there are <u>no mistakes</u>.

Glossary

Adjective	A word that modifies a noun, e.g. <u>small</u> barn, <u>hot</u> tea.
Adverb	A word that describes a verb, e.g. walk <u>slowly</u>, shout <u>loudly</u>.
Apostrophe	Used to show <u>missing letters</u> and <u>belonging</u> (possession). $\boxed{\text{ʼ}}$
Brackets	Used to separate <u>extra information</u> in a sentence. $\boxed{\text{( )}}$
Clause	A bit of a sentence that contains <u>a subject</u> and <u>a verb</u>.
Colon	Used to introduce extra information (e.g. a <u>list</u>) and join <u>sentences</u>. $\boxed{:}$
Comma	Separates items in a <u>list</u>, <u>extra information</u>, and <u>joins clauses</u>. $\boxed{,}$
Conjunction	A word or words used to <u>link</u> two <u>clauses</u> or <u>sentences</u>, e.g. <u>and</u>, <u>however</u>.
Dash	Separates <u>extra information</u> in a sentence or introduces a pause. $\boxed{—}$
Direct speech	The <u>actual</u> words that are <u>said</u> by someone.
Inverted commas	Used to show <u>direct speech</u> (also called speech marks). $\boxed{\text{“ ”}}$
Main clause	An <u>important</u> bit of a sentence that would <u>make sense</u> on its own, e.g. <u>We played golf</u> while they watched. 'We played golf' is the <u>main clause</u>.
Noun	A word that <u>names</u> something, e.g. <u>Roger</u>, <u>chocolate</u>, <u>bunch</u>, <u>joy</u>.
Phrase	<u>Part</u> of a sentence, which <u>either</u> doesn't have a <u>verb</u>, or doesn't have a <u>subject</u> (some phrases might have <u>neither</u>).
Prefix	<u>Letters</u> that can be put <u>in front</u> of a word to change its meaning, e.g. <u>un</u>do.
Preposition	A word that tells you <u>how</u> things are <u>related</u>, e.g. <u>at</u>, <u>over</u>, <u>under</u>.
Pronoun	A word that can be used <u>instead of a noun</u>, e.g. <u>I</u>, <u>you</u>, <u>he</u>, <u>it</u>.
Reported speech	What someone has said, but <u>not</u> in their <u>own words</u>.
Semicolon	Used to separate <u>lists</u> of longer things and <u>join</u> sentences. $\boxed{;}$
Subordinate clause	An <u>extra</u> bit of a sentence which <u>couldn't be a full sentence</u> on its own, e.g. <u>After they left</u>, she cried. 'After they left' is the <u>subordinate clause</u>.
Suffix	Letters that can be put <u>after</u> a word to change its meaning, e.g. joy<u>ful</u>.
Verb	A <u>doing</u> or <u>being</u> word, e.g. I <u>walk</u>, you <u>left</u>, he <u>is</u>.

Answers

Section One — Spelling Rules

Q1 a) hous<u>es</u> d) church<u>es</u>
b) fox<u>es</u> e) carrot<u>s</u>
c) glass<u>es</u>

Q2 a) berr<u>ies</u> d) bab<u>ies</u>
b) day<u>s</u> e) part<u>ies</u>
c) boy<u>s</u>

Q3 a) radio<u>s</u> d) hero<u>es</u>
b) photo<u>s</u> e) rhino<u>s</u>
c) tomato<u>es</u>

Q4 a) loa<u>ves</u> d) thie<u>ves</u>
b) belief<u>s</u> e) kni<u>ves</u>
c) wi<u>ves</u>

Q5 a) sheep ('sheep' is the same in its singular and plural form).
b) child<u>ren</u> d) g<u>ee</u>se
c) wom<u>e</u>n e) t<u>ee</u>th

Q6 a) <u>im</u>perfect d) <u>il</u>literate
b) <u>ir</u>relevant e) <u>un</u>necessary
c) <u>re</u>use

Q7 a) cheer<u>ful</u> d) sens<u>ible</u>
b) valu<u>able</u> e) common<u>ly</u>
c) care<u>ful</u>

Q8 a) happ<u>ily</u> d) funn<u>ily</u>
b) soft<u>ly</u> e) normal<u>ly</u>
c) gent<u>ly</u>

Q9 a) env<u>ious</u> d) funn<u>ier</u>
b) merci<u>ful</u> e) try<u>ing</u>
c) delay<u>ed</u>

Q10 a) thin<u>ner</u> d) challeng<u>er</u>
b) dump<u>ed</u> e) chatt<u>ing</u>
c) talk<u>ing</u>

Q11 a) My dog is the <u>worst</u> dog at puppy training. Hopefully he'll behave <u>better</u> one day.
b) Sayid is <u>taller</u> than Herbert, but he eats <u>less</u> than him.

Q12 a) <u>s</u>cissors d) whis<u>t</u>le
b) <u>k</u>nowledge e) answer
c) <u>g</u>host f) bom<u>b</u>

Q13 a) doct<u>o</u>r d) anim<u>a</u>l
b) priv<u>a</u>te e) govern<u>m</u>ent
c) fright<u>e</u>ned f) bisc<u>u</u>it

Q14 a) <u>c</u>ity c) mus<u>c</u>le
b) <u>c</u>ircle d) <u>c</u>entury

Q15 Our TV broke, so we took it back to the shop with the rec<u>ei</u>pt. We got a new one (big enough to reach the c<u>ei</u>ling), but the next day a th<u>ie</u>f broke in and stole it. I can't bel<u>ie</u>ve our luck!

Q16 Mike, my best fr<u>ie</u>nd, is great, but he's also really w<u>ei</u>rd and he's beginn<u>i</u>ng to get on my nerves. He loves celebrit<u>ie</u>s and talks about them all the time at s<u>c</u>hool, espe<u>c</u>ially when we're in s<u>c</u>ience — it's very distract<u>ing</u>.

Section Two — Common Spelling Mistakes

Q1 a) <u>Maybe</u> George is a superhero.
b) That <u>may be</u> true.

Q2 Is there <u>any way</u> we could go to the cinema for my party? It's a great idea because <u>everybody</u> loves films. If no one wants to come, we could just go <u>anyway</u>.

Q3 <u>In fact</u> I have got <u>a lot</u> to say <u>thank you</u> for.

Q4 I really want my brother to get his driving <u>licence</u> so he can drive me to netball <u>practice</u>. My <u>advice</u> to him is to <u>practise</u> as much as possible.

Q5 Judy has just <u>passed</u> her driving test. In the <u>past</u> she took the bus.

Q6 a) I hate the <u>effect</u> sad films have on me.
b) This might <u>affect</u> you.

Q7 Tom won't <u>accept</u> any criticism, <u>except</u> from his brother.

Q8 a) <u>Where</u> are the doughnuts?
b) We <u>were</u> only joking.
c) You're not allowed to <u>wear</u> make-up at school.
d) I didn't know <u>where</u> we <u>were</u>.

Q9 a) The monkeys have taken <u>their</u> windscreen wipers.
b) They went over <u>there</u>.
c) <u>They're</u> so cute.

Q10 <u>You're</u> a scruffy so-and-so. Just look at <u>your</u> hair!

Q11 a) My gran can't <u>hear</u> very well.
b) I don't like it <u>here</u>.

Q12 <u>Two</u> chipmunks set off <u>to</u> the zoo. A squirrel shouted, "Can I come <u>too</u>?"

Q13 a) Rahul isn't very <u>thorough</u> in his work.
b) I like his clothes. I don't get his hairstyle <u>though</u>.
c) Please go <u>through</u> to the kitchen.

Q14 I'm not sure <u>whether</u> that <u>piece</u> of cake will help Don <u>lose</u> weight.

Q15 I want to <u>buy</u> a painting <u>by</u> a local artist, but he just can't say good<u>bye</u> to it.

Q16 a) Can you <u>teach</u> me to dance?
b) I need to <u>borrow</u> your cookery book.

Q17 a) Tilly <u>bought</u> a new bike with her pocket money.
b) Sorry Sir, I haven't <u>brought</u> my P.E. kit today.

Q18 a) ini<u>tial</u> e) streng<u>th</u>
b) g<u>u</u>est f) <u>tough</u>
c) cau<u>tious</u> g) q<u>u</u>est
d) fic<u>tion</u> h) r<u>h</u>ythm

Section Three — Punctuation

Q1 <u>O</u>n <u>M</u>onday, <u>I</u> met a <u>S</u>panish man named <u>J</u>avier at the beach.

Q2 a) <u>I</u> went to the zoo on <u>F</u>riday<u>.</u>
b) <u>C</u>ould <u>I</u> borrow some milk<u>?</u>
c) <u>T</u>he dog licked <u>T</u>im<u>.</u>

Q3 a) Yesterday, I saw pigs<u>,</u> cows<u>,</u> sheep and a giant turnip.
b) I bought a washing line<u>,</u> three potatoes<u>,</u> a calculator and twenty napkins.

Q4 a) Georgia enjoyed the film<u>,</u> but Beth thought it was boring.
b) The dog needed a walk<u>,</u> so Jill took her out on the fields.

Q5 a) Ian and Lesley<u>,</u> our neighbours<u>,</u> like to go on holiday to Greece.
b) Carol<u>,</u> who loves movies<u>,</u> has just made her own action film.

Q6 At the weekend Franz went skiing, swimming and horse riding<u>;</u> he bought a hovercraft, a bouncy castle and a banjo<u>;</u> and he prepared a three-course meal of soup, pasta and jelly.

Q7 a) The police need new helmets<u>:</u> sandwiches no longer fit under their old ones.
b) Some people like a quiet life<u>;</u> others are big risk-takers.

Q8 a) Sadie<u>'</u>s favourite meal is a roast dinner <u>(</u>specifically roast beef<u>)</u>.
b) The C.S.A.S. <u>(</u>Coffee Shop Appreciation Society<u>)</u> is a great place for coffee fans.

Q9 a) I played squash every day <u>—</u> until I broke my arm.
b) The winners <u>—</u> Lee and Mark <u>—</u> stood up.

Q10 a) The fire-breathing dragon's father-in-law had just turned sixty-six.
b) Luisa was the editor of a pro-American magazine.

Q11 a) <u>I'm</u> going out.
b) She <u>won't</u> like it.
c) <u>They're</u> too big.
d) <u>We've</u> arrived.

Q12 a) Joanne never <u>lets</u> me win.
b) <u>Let's</u> have spaghetti tonight.

Q13 a) The <u>mayor's</u> wife was not impressed.
b) The <u>church's</u> steeple is wonky.
c) Jacob watched as the <u>men's</u> bus drove off.
d) The <u>pupils'</u> noses all turned blue.

Q14 a) <u>It's</u> time to go home.
b) <u>It's</u> three o'clock.
c) The cat chased <u>its</u> tail.

Q15 a) Brian asked<u>,</u> <u>"W</u>hat happens if I press this button<u>?"</u>
b) <u>"</u>The world will end<u>,"</u> replied Nadeen<u>.</u>

Section Four — Grammar: Basics

Q1 <u>Proper nouns</u> — Mr Smith, December
<u>Common nouns</u> — horse, chimney
<u>Abstract nouns</u> — freedom

Q2 a) <u>a</u> company **d)** <u>a</u> unicorn
b) <u>an</u> igloo **e)** <u>a</u> newspaper
c) <u>an</u> umbrella

Q3 a) <u>She</u> likes <u>it</u>.
b) Those are <u>his</u>.
c) <u>They</u> eat <u>them</u>.
d) His hand touched <u>hers</u>.
e) <u>He</u> looks at <u>her</u>.
f) That's not <u>yours</u>.

Q4 a) Pam and <u>I</u> left.
b) Kareem gave <u>me</u> a pen.
c) Tell <u>me</u> the truth.

Q5 a) Henry had a friend <u>who</u> was called Percy.
b) I've got an itch <u>which</u> is just out of reach.

Q6 a) Bill is the man <u>who</u> buys the milk.
b) To <u>whom</u> did you write?

Q7 a) <u>Who's</u> going to the party?
b) <u>Whose</u> bag is this?

Q8 a) I <u>chase</u> rabbits in the park.
b) She <u>likes</u> chocolate.
c) We <u>sing</u> carols.

Q9 a) Sarah has straight<u>,</u> light blonde hair.
b) Big<u>,</u> grumpy<u>,</u> fluffy lions are watching me.

Q10 'Badly', 'crazily' and 'very' are <u>adverbs</u>.
'Friendly' and 'silly' are <u>adjectives</u>.

Q11 a) 'He made a cake.' is a sentence.
b) 'At six o'clock.' is not a sentence.
c) 'Tell me more.' is a sentence.
d) 'Not now.' is not a sentence.

Q12 a) 'In the dark' is a phrase.
b) 'By himself' is a phrase.
c) 'Karl tickles Snowy' is a clause.
d) 'Take me home' is a clause.

Q13 a) 'Sid plays golf' is a main clause.
b) 'Because of the sun' is a subordinate clause.
c) 'Whilst singing' is a subordinate clause.
d) 'They fell down' is a main clause.

Q14 Our kitchen is a mess. There are dirty dishes <u>in</u> the sink and boxes <u>on</u> the floor. It's been like this <u>since</u> March. There's no space for us to cook <u>at</u> teatime.

Q15 For, And, Nor, But, Or, Yet and So.

Q16 The biggest challenge facing Junior League Football today is the sheer number of red and yellow cards issued by referees. There is no doubt that standards of discipline have fallen sharply.
Last year, 85 yellow cards and 14 red cards were issued in the first six weeks of the season. In comparison, 136 yellow cards and 26 red cards have already been issued this year. Many players are facing a four-match ban.
Hector Dalrymple, Chairman of the UK Federation of Under-16 Football Clubs, claimed the situation was reaching crisis point.

Q17 a) There <u>isn't any</u> food in the fridge.
b) I <u>don't</u> know.
c) She <u>doesn't</u> work here.

Section Five — Grammar: Tenses

Q1 a) There <u>was</u> an earthquake — <u>past tense</u>.
b) I <u>will visit</u> Granny tomorrow — <u>future tense</u>.
c) Andy <u>plays</u> volleyball — <u>present tense</u>.

Q2 a) Kareema <u>goes</u> to badminton club.
b) Mrs Tunstall <u>bakes</u> delicious cakes.
c) I <u>have</u> a sore throat.
d) A butterfly <u>flies</u> around our garden.
e) Happiness <u>is</u> the key to success.
f) Frogs <u>swim</u> in our pond.

Q3 a) Mrs Busy-Body <u>is peeping</u> over the fence.
b) Miss Obedient <u>is agreeing</u> with you.
c) Lady Tango <u>is dancing</u> to music.
d) Mr Outdoorsy <u>is walking</u> to the park.
e) Master Scout <u>is planning</u> his route.
f) Sir Fibber <u>is lying</u> to his wife.

Q4 a) I <u>stopped</u> the car.
b) Sheila <u>cleaned</u> her desk.
c) Oscar <u>saw</u> his teacher dancing.
d) They <u>changed</u> their clothes.
e) My brother <u>lent</u> me his bike.
f) Kam <u>went</u> to London last week.
g) The pop stars <u>met</u> their fans.
h) We <u>cut</u> our hair last night.

Q5 a) Miriam <u>has hit</u> Alf.
b) We <u>have gone</u> to bed.
c) The birds <u>have eaten</u> the seeds.
d) The boys <u>have climbed</u> the tree.
e) Mustafa <u>has played</u> cards.
f) Tyrone <u>has written</u> a letter.

Q6 a) They <u>have seen</u> / <u>saw</u> the film.
b) I <u>have done</u> / <u>did</u> all my work.
c) Franklin and Geoff <u>have been</u> swimming.
d) Mr Potts <u>has done</u> / <u>did</u> the housework.
e) Jared <u>has seen</u> / <u>saw</u> the new plans.
f) <u>Have you done</u> / <u>Did you do</u> the washing.

Q7 a) Faye was <u>being</u> very silly.
b) Dev was just <u>being</u> awkward.
c) The children were <u>seeing</u> Granny.
d) The judges have <u>seen</u> the band.

Q8 a) Simon thought <u>of</u> a great idea.
b) The fans should <u>have</u> shouted more.
c) The party may <u>have</u> been cancelled.
d) The opposition could <u>have</u> tried harder.
e) He's never heard <u>of</u> that.
f) The winners might <u>have</u> celebrated.

Q9 Last year we went to Madrid and we <u>visited</u> my friends. We swam in their pool, <u>played</u> tennis and <u>ate</u> paella. We <u>saw</u> the opera house and the cathedral. My sister and I took a trip on the city tour bus. When we got off, we <u>looked</u> around the 'Museo del Prado' (a big art gallery). I spoke a bit of Spanish and <u>tried</u> lots of different food. I also met lots of people and <u>made</u> lots of new friends. It was a great trip!

Index